CW01314035

So You Want to Be a
STREET PREACHER

Jimmy Hamilton

WESTBOW
PRESS®
A DIVISION OF THOMAS NELSON
& ZONDERVAN

Copyright © 2020 Jimmy Hamilton.

All rights reserved. No part of this book may be used or reproduced by any means, graphic, electronic, or mechanical, including photocopying, recording, taping or by any information storage retrieval system without the written permission of the author except in the case of brief quotations embodied in critical articles and reviews.

This book is a work of non-fiction. Unless otherwise noted, the author and the publisher make no explicit guarantees as to the accuracy of the information contained in this book and in some cases, names of people and places have been altered to protect their privacy.

WestBow Press books may be ordered through booksellers or by contacting:

WestBow Press
A Division of Thomas Nelson & Zondervan
1663 Liberty Drive
Bloomington, IN 47403
www.westbowpress.com
1 (866) 928-1240

Because of the dynamic nature of the Internet, any web addresses or links contained in this book may have changed since publication and may no longer be valid. The views expressed in this work are solely those of the author and do not necessarily reflect the views of the publisher, and the publisher hereby disclaims any responsibility for them.

Any people depicted in stock imagery provided by Getty Images are models, and such images are being used for illustrative purposes only. Certain stock imagery © Getty Images.

Scripture taken from the King James Version of the Bible.

ISBN: 978-1-9736-8174-8 (sc)
ISBN: 978-1-9736-8176-2 (hc)
ISBN: 978-1-9736-8175-5 (e)

Library of Congress Control Number: 2019920680

Print information available on the last page.

WestBow Press rev. date: 12/18/2019

Dedicated to the memory of Pastor Paul Schneider (1897-1939) 'The Pastor of Buchenwald'.

"He has courage who is completely set free from himself and only he has it" (P. Schneider)

Foreword

No biblical ministry is easy, but this is especially so for street preaching. Criticism comes from all directions, regardless of how you go about it. Then there are the physical elements of heat, cold, and rain, not to mention the wear and tear on the voice, and the exhaustion that sets in after being on your feet half the day. Nowadays there are also police to worry about, and soon enough there will be stones and martyrdom. There is nothing easy about street preaching—so the question is, why do it? As the following book will demonstrate, when you've been called by the Lord, you can't help but go and do it. Like Jeremiah, some men have been raised up who realise there is a fire in their bones and they go and proclaim. Through trials and tears, through criticism and rough weather, through ostracism and arrests, still these men will know their greatest joy when they are heralding the things of Christ to an adulterous generation. This is why the following book is so vital. The street preacher needs to know what he's getting himself into. Many pastors and churches, as helpful as they usually are, don't know what to do with street preachers. This is not to criticise church leaders, but rather to point out that here, in the following pages, the street preacher will be exposed to practical advice on how to go about his calling from someone who has been preaching on the streets for roughly four decades, in all kinds of weather, in many parts of the world, both as pastor and evangelist. Jimmy Hamilton is one of the most faithful, humble ministers ever to herald the gospel. If anyone were to write such a guide for street preachers, he is one of the most qualified to do so. Also, the street preacher needs encouragement. Most who read this book have perhaps already preached in the open air. They have already experienced the travail of the battle. This is exactly why such persons need to read this book. Here you'll find stories to refresh your soul; you'll find advice that'll be a balm for your wounds. Every page will resonate with your own experiences, which is a sweet encouragement for the street preacher who, sadly enough, rarely finds brethren who gets it or who gets him. Give yourselves a blessing and read this book—and share it with others, whether or not they are street preachers. This is a trusty battle manual that needs to be in every Christian's library. I couldn't recommend it enough.

(Ryan Denton, Christ in the Wild Ministries)
www.christinthewild.com

(Ryan Denton is a former pastor, presently involved in evangelistic labours in El Paso, Texas bringing the gospel to both the streets and the campuses in Texas. He is also a co-author of *'A Certain Sound': Christian Heritage Publications).*

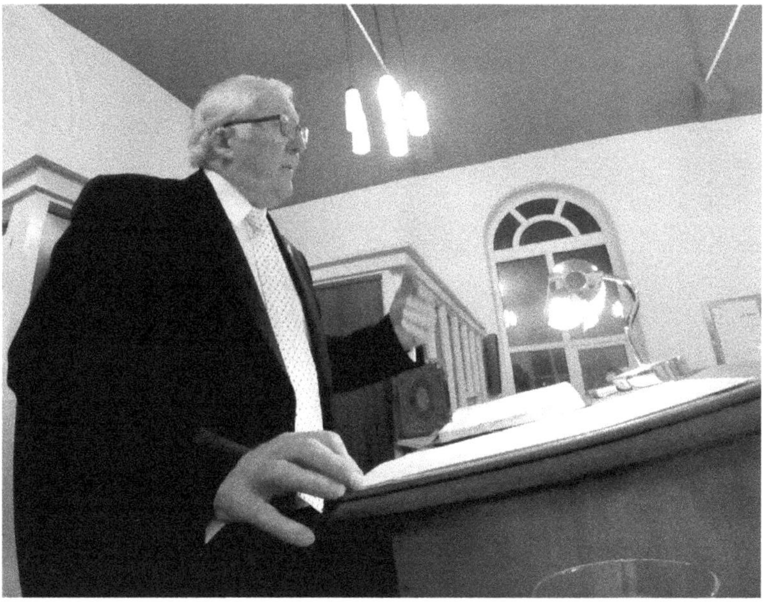

Introduction

Let it be stated from the outset, this book is not written for theologians nor ordained ministers. It is mainly written for young men who believe they have a gift to preach God's Word and desire to reach the lost of this world. It is argued by some within our Reformed fraternity (See Appendix 1) that there is no such office as that of an evangelist, and that only ordained ministers ought to be preaching the gospel. This view came about as a result of a myriad of itinerant preachers that arose on the back of the Reformation. Many, who, to say the least, were less than helpful. It could be argued that that is the case even today. I fully understand this, and it's one of the reasons I write this book. The only way to rise above this is to ensure that we, who are committed to and involved in street preaching ministry, raise our game and seek to dispel this fear amongst our brethren. How? By soundness in doctrine and life, and especially by our conduct in the public arena.

I think it can be argued that there is a place even yet, as there was in the New Testament, for an itinerant (Περιπατητικός) preaching ministry. It certainly could be argued that amidst the dreadful apostasy and confusion that we are faced with, particularly in Europe and the West in general, that there is a great need for more and more gospel workers. But is a title, an office, necessary for such workers? I prefer simply the title 'Gospel Workers' as per the *"Church Order commentary of Dordrecht"*. Some may prefer the title 'Missionary'. It was said by the late Dr M.L-Jones that all evangelism should be accomplished by and through the local church, to which I would heartily agree; but, sadly, it is most often not done by the local church. One can hardly blame men who aspire to reach the lost with the gifts that they have, when faced with such apathy and lack of zeal and intent within the churches, if they go off on their own. This book is not written to inculcate rebellion nor to encourage mavericks, but to help sincere and godly young men, rather than just leaving them to their own devices. Surely it would be better for our churches and ministers to instruct, disciple and equip such young men to do their work in an educated, biblical, godly and responsible fashion, with the authority and blessing of their church rather than without it. Instead I perceive that many are just going to go ahead and do it anyway. In my own time in pastoral ministry, I would like to have had such men with these aspirations. I most certainly would not have held them back, but rather encouraged and helped them in every way I possibly could. I certainly wouldn't have seen them as a threat to my position. For my part, I desire to see an army of such men, armed and equipped with good doctrine, and in the power of the Holy Spirit going where the Lord would take them, with the gospel of Jesus Christ. I cannot but think that would be pleasing to Him—but with the blessing and under the authority of their local church.

Some are opposed to this ministry who would argue that there is no biblical warrant for it. I would ask them to think again. In Luke's gospel, we have the words (and therefore the authority) of the Lord Jesus Christ himself saying, *"But into whatsoever city ye enter, and they receive you not, go your ways out into the streets of the same, and say..."* (Luke 10:10). In verse one of that chapter, Jesus sends, not just his twelve disciples, but seventy of his other followers to preach. You could argue that the twelve apostles were the ordained ministers, and the seventy workers were given to supplement their labours. They were sent directly by the Lord Jesus Christ himself. The New Testament canon, of course, did not exist at this point in redemptive history.

So, what were the instructions of Christ to these men? He sent them in twos, which is very wise, as a man in Satan's territory needs someone to watch his back. To have a fellow worker is most useful. If one is discouraged the other lifts him up; if one is erring the other can correct him; one may see the danger while the other does not; and two witnesses can confirm a matter when controversy or trouble arises—but alas, some of us would never get anything done at all if we had to wait for another workman. Scripture presents us with the ideal, the perfect, to which we are ever straining towards, but we toil in the midst of the imperfect. The number seventy is not necessarily exact. It is, however, a perfect number. The number seven, biblically, signifies the fullness of the covenant of grace; so thus compounded, seventy would signify fullness, a complete number.

Should not such workers be expected and found in our churches today, apart that is from the ordained ministers, elders and deacons? Is it possible that they are there but we, and even the potential workers themselves, are unaware of the fact? Are we failing to train and equip people for the Lord's service as we ought to be? Was this not an integral part of the Lord's ministry and that of his apostles? As Jesus himself preached, he called men to himself, not just to occupy pews on the Sabbath day (Mark 1:14-20). He had a work for them to do, so he not only called them but he taught and trained them—on-the-job training. It was while in their secular employment and under the ministry of the Word that these men were called to serve (Luke 5.1-11). Simon (Peter) and Andrew were the first. Now they must lay aside their fishing labours and take up a ministry of fishing for men (v17).

There are four important points we need to see here.

The first is that a big part of the Lord's ministry was directed in teaching others to carry on the work of the gospel, that good news they are to carry forward into the world (Acts 1.8). Surely that is a principle we need to be more aware of in our churches: on-the-job training. It was alongside the Lord these men were able to learn, to make the most of their mistakes and be better instructed, grapple with their misunderstandings, and eventually be equipped to go on with their given task. Surely that ought to be an integral part of Christian, that is church, ministry today? If churches were growing and developing the talent that they have, instilling in members the ability to confess their Lord and the confidence to defend the faith, surely local communities could be turned upside down.

A second point that needs to be made clear is that these men were not smart, clever, learned men. That is not the criteria for ministry. Now we're not praising ignorance. Learning is valuable, and it is imperative for any ministry. But surely it is godliness, holiness of life, closeness to Jesus, and hearts gripped with truth and a passion for the souls of lost men that is much more important. Jesus can work wonders with very ordinary folk.

The third point is that these men are not layabouts with nothing else to do. They are hard-working men, skilled in the fishing trade, when they were sent. I think a man should be able to show that he can hold down a job before he enters into Christian work of any kind.

A fourth and important point is that it is that they are called to serve while under the ministry of the Word (Luke 5.1-3). That is how a person will be called by God. If a man has no time for the Bible, either reading it for himself or sitting under the authority of the Word of God, he has no place in any ministry. When I say that these were not clever men, there was no doubt they had a desire to learn, and so there will be in anyone called to serve God.

We are commanded to pray the Lord to raise these gospel workers in our day (Luke 10:2; Matthew 9.35-38). Why? Because there is a harvest and the labourers are few, always few—but that doesn't mean there are none.

They had to go trusting, in faith (Luke 10:3), because they were going amongst wolves. They would be faced with great hostility (something many of our fine pulpiteers today know nothing of). The gospel workers must be willing to accept whatever hospitality is offered to them as worthy recipients (Luke 10:7; Matthew 10:10;

1 Corinthians 9:14). They are instructed as to what to preach—the kingdom of God (Luke 10:9). They could do so because the King himself had come: he was near. They were to preach, warning the people of the catastrophic judgment that would be visited upon despisers of their message (Luke 10:16), and they were to give examples of past judgments, such as Sodom and others. This, I remind you, is on the streets, amid the general public, not in the comfort of a local church building where all are supposedly Christian.

Such preaching is seldom heard in today's declining Christendom. Love warns. It is a lack of love that knows that such profound judgment is coming upon men and women the world over but, whether out of fear, embarrassment, or politeness, refuses to warn people. The preaching of Hell is imperative. To argue that such a ministry is not biblical is hardly intelligent. To argue further that all preaching should be reserved for churches and pulpits is certainly not in any way justifiable from the Bible; and to argue that seventy men who had never been to a seminary, had only sat under one minister, and that for a short space of time, were hardly qualified for such a task, doesn't fit the biblical record here either. These men had only heard him, Christ. They had no church membership, no college or seminary degrees, and they had never had hands laid on by other men. Finally, these men were sent into the darkness of a spiritually hardened Israel. Who in their right mind could argue that such ministry is not needed in the ever-increasing decline in the entirety of Europe and the West today?

I pray, *"Lord, please, raise up not seventy, but seventy times seventy such gospel workers in our churches and nations today. .Send them out on to the streets to lift up thy name. And Lord, open the eyes of our churches, not only to see that the harvest is great, but to see the talent already in their midst, waiting to be trained, equipped and sent out to work. Amen."*

The church is gathered from the four corners of the earth by the preaching in every age. The preaching reaches those whom God intends it to reach, not every man head for head. The content of preaching is the gospel, nothing else. The result of preaching is either the regeneration, repentance and faith required for salvation, or the hardening of sinners' hearts: it will accomplish one or the other.

"To the one we are the savour of death unto death; and to the other the savour of life unto life. And who is sufficient for these things" (2 Corinthians 2:16)?"

"Every time God's Word is proclaimed it changes all of those within its hearing. No one ever remains unaffected by God's Word. To those who hear it positively, there is growth in grace. To those who reject it or are indifferent to it, calluses are added to their souls and calcium to their hearts. The eye becomes dimmer and dimmer, the ear heavier and heavier, and the mystery of the kingdom more and more obscure. He who has ears to hear, let him hear" (R.C. Sproul).

Those who are saved are brought to faith as a result of God's choosing, will, method, message and operations, not by the will of man himself nor the preacher's either. God's method of gathering his church is the preaching of his Word, watered by the prayers of his people. Not much of the preaching that we encounter in the Bible was done in church buildings. It took place in synagogues sometimes, but also in houses, in boats, on hillsides, *and on the street*. The church throughout the ages has had a history of street preaching. I am convinced that street preaching is unarguably a biblical method. It is not the *only* method, but it is a most excellent one for reaching the lost for Christ with the instrument of his holy and divine Word. A lady whose minister had just moved on lamented, "I don't know what we'll do without him. He used to explain the Bible to us." What an epitaph! That is the preacher's task.

To preach the gospel is to engage in evangelism: it is to bring good news to people. To be a preacher is to be a messenger, a man with a message from God that has first of all transformed him and is now like a fire in his bosom. He is not just any messenger. He is a herald, commissioned by the King to deliver his message. He has no authority unless he has been sent. Nor is he allowed to add or to take away anything from the King's message. He is accountable to the King. The vital thing regarding preaching is that in it people hear the voice of the King, Christ himself (John 10:27). They hear his voice in preaching (Romans 1:16-17; Romans 10:13-14; 1 Corinthians 1:18, 23-24; Ephesians 2:17). In preaching, it is Christ who comes and preaches, *"peace to you which were afar off, and to them that were nigh"* (Ephesians 2:17). That is because Christ is in the preaching, his voice is heard. *"It is the power of God unto salvation to every one that believeth"* (Romans 1:16); and it is the wisdom of God (1 Corinthians 1:23-24) and that is why it saves.

Before a man can preach to others, he of course must first be converted himself and be personally godly. This is one of the reasons why *ideally* the preacher should be sent by his church. Whether the task is undertaken in a church building or a market square, it is a sacred, deeply solemn and holy task. It is not a task for the foolish and ignorant. To deliver the King's message he must know the King's message. He is not there to tell jokes, entertain, or to perform theatrics, but with the utmost seriousness to preach the counsel of God. Therefore, conversion and personal godliness are an indispensable prerequisite. Also, a good knowledge of Scripture and its doctrines is essential—the sovereignty of God and of his grace, and justification by faith alone, apart from works—but with an utter dependence upon God, for, *"who is sufficient for these things"* (2 Corinthians 2:16)?

Conversion & Calling

I've been a street preacher for thirty-eight of my forty years as a Christian. In coming to Christ I was broken, in great distress. I called upon his name and he rescued me (See Appendix 3).

I once walked in fear, in darkness,
Held captive and broken by sin;

Of God and His Son so careless,
Until Jesus and light entered in.
My God knew my pain and my sadness,
Each detail of heart and life;
Yet showed me his utter kindness,
And brought me such sweet relief.

I once was held fast in sin's power,
Which ruled me and kept me in chains;
But Jesus He came and to conquer,
His grace he poured into my veins.
I tried and I tried to get freedom,
I cried and I cried for some peace;
Then, Jesus, He came with His pardon,
From judgment, He gave me release.

How can I forget that sweet tone,
You're free, yes, you are really free;
You'll never again be all alone,
Today He is still walking with me.
He lifted me out of my bondage,
From the filth and the mire of sin;
He's mine till the end of the ages,
And mine through the ages of heav'n.

(Tune: Crugybar 9 8. 9 8. D anapaestic)
(© James R. Hamilton – Written 31st December 2003)

From the very beginning, I had an all-consuming desire to tell others of what Jesus had done for me and to speak to others of this phenomenal message of God's Word. But my big question was how to do it. I was in what could only be described as a very respectable, middle-class church, whose teaching was somewhat superficial, not to mention theologically Arminian. The church's views on street preaching were discouraging also. I began to study on my own, via distance learning courses with the Bible Training Institute in my native city of Glasgow, in Scotland. I studied doctrine, coming to see the Reformed exposition as being thoroughly biblical. I studied church history, seeing a heritage of men who didn't just sit behind a pulpit desk but took the gospel to the people on the street. The more I learned the hungrier I became and the more I was consumed with a desire to take the gospel to the streets. I was denounced from the pulpit by one of the church's elders for my preaching on the street, but I was not in any way daunted. The more that came against me the more determined I was to persist. I knew from Scripture and from my studies of history and preaching itself that this was what was needed. And I had the inner conviction of the Holy Spirit that this was the way for me. I was preaching on the street in Stafford town on one occasion with one or two other church members present. As I opened my mouth to speak, though naturally very shy and timid, I became very conscious of the energy of the Holy Spirit deeply influencing my preaching; I was enabled to explain the gospel very boldly and as never before. I came away from that experience knowing that this was my calling.

Desire & Development

So why am I telling you all this? Well, if you're going to be a street preacher there are some things you need to be certain of before you begin. First, that you are a Christian; that you have been reborn of the Spirit of God, and that your entire being has been radically altered by the supernatural power of Almighty God. Second, if you have a desire to preach the Word of God, you will have a desire to study and learn the Word of God. If this is of no interest to you, then forget it: you are not called to preach God's Word. You may not have the best church, or the best teachers in the world, but you will find a way to overcome and to learn, to equip yourself. To be as well-grounded in the truth of God's Word as you possibly can is a necessity if you are to make it known to others. Are you articulate? I mean, can you give clear, simple directions as to how a person might get from A to B? If you have trouble doing that, then how will you be able to direct a sinner to the cross?

If God sets someone to the doing of something, whatever it be, and there is a desire to obey, there will be opposition, and that opposition will sometimes come from the most unlikely sources. In undertaking a street ministry, you are about to step out into Satan's territory, and he is one mean piece of work. What if the opposition comes from within, or from family, church or fellow believers? The same principles apply to this as do for discipleship (Luke 14:25-33). You need to know you are of God, that you have God's calling; and you need his grace to begin and to persevere, or you will make yourself a laughingstock. I had to wait nearly five years before my course was vindicated by the Lord. Eventually, I had to leave my first church, not because they didn't like what I was doing, but because they turned in an unacceptable ecumenical direction. My new church, along with minister and officers, immediately recognised my gift and calling and I was sent by that church to minister God's Word.

Two Indicators of a Man's Calling to Preach

The Old Testament prophets and the New Testament apostles were called and sent forth by God directly (Isaiah 6:8; Jeremiah 1:1; Romans 1:1; Ephesians 1:1). The apostles had helpers who also were called *'Ministers of Christ'* (Colossians 1:7) and *'Servants of Christ'* (2 Corinthians 5:20). *"All believers have a calling to preach or to witness"* (H. Bavinck), but to have a definite charge with authority, within an office, over a congregation, a man must be elected and appointed (Romans 10:15).

"Therefore every one must take heed, not to intrude himself by

indecent means, but is bound to wait till it shall please God to call him; that he may have the testimony of his calling, and be certain and assured that it is of the Lord" (Belgic Confession of Faith).

A man must not assume this authority upon his own (Hebrews 5:4). Since the call is no longer given directly and extraordinarily, God now uses means, including both an internal and an external calling.

The former is somewhat subjective. There is a personal conviction in a man's heart that God would have him to preach. He will know a consistent love for the gospel ministry, accompanied by a desire to serve the God who loved and saved both he and his people. This is given birth to in prayerful meditation. Then there is the question of ability, not only strength of body and character but of mind and speech. He will have to deny himself and be willing to serve Christ where, when and however he would have him. Now, don't just skim over these matters with a nod of approval. Think about them. Are you willing to submit, to yield yourself in all these areas? This is internal, and you alone can answer yes or no. To what end do you wish to enter the gospel ministry? To escape the toils of manual labour? Or is it just another form of livelihood? Is your desire to glorify God, to see his kingdom extended, his people gathered in? What of the ways and means? Is the way open? If not then maybe the answer is no, you are not called, for now at least.

But how is the internal call ratified, for we can hardly trust ourselves, our feelings and our hearts (Jeremiah 17:9)? Hence the external call. The external call comes to us through the instrumentality of our church, its ministry, officers etc. How this works out in practice will vary according to a particular church or denomination. The lack of an external call can be a problem. It's the problem of authority, or rather the lack thereof. Other believers also may affirm or deny our perceived calling. I say, ideally, as there are always exceptions and we will come to that.

When it comes to a church affirming a man's calling to preach, what are they be looking for essentially? Well, they would be looking with both fasting and prayer, for this is no small matter they are about. They will take into consideration the man's knowledge of Scripture, and his theology, that he has a good grasp of both, with the ability to open the Word of God and deal with controversies; and that he is well-grounded in the tenets of the Reformed faith. They would be considering how he has practiced what he believes within the body of Christ during the time he has been with them, that his life matches his faith. Then they would doubtless have heard him preach, and that more than once. What did they hear? A man preaching the Word, breaking open the bread of life to them? Did he simply tell them what they wanted to hear, or did he apply the truth to their consciences, challenging them concerning sin, righteousness and judgment? Did he preach Christ and him crucified? Did he break them down and build them up? Did he exhort, encourage, pour in the balm of Gilead? Did he preach seriously, or was he lighthearted, a joker even? Or was it a lecture? Perhaps they would consider his knowledge of church history also, the historic Confessions of the Christian faith, and how through the sufferings of our brethren past we have the truth systemised and handed on a plate for us today.

Then they would most certainly consider his ethics. You might say that if his moral standing is shaky should he be a member of the church, never mind be preaching? And rightly so. But in today's climate with such decline in Western churches, even Reformed ones, ethical standards are often wanting. How often the Lord's name has been tarnished by men who have failed in this realm. These ethical standards can no longer be simply assumed while we are in the midst of a sexual revolution that is pandemic. These are no longer private matters for an individual who is about to be sent into the public domain to preach and represent not just the church, but Jesus Christ himself.

So, the church would be looking for an exceptional man. He is godly, has a reverence for God and the things of God. He has a humility of heart and a very high and strict standard of morality. In other words, he would be a man of discretion, clarity, soundness of judgment and discernment. If he lacks these qualities, it does not matter how eloquently he can communicate. One of the great benefits of a man who has been affirmed by an external call is the power, the authority it gives him. He goes out knowing he hasn't gone off on his own steam. He is there because he has been sent by the Lord, and the Lord's people have affirmed that calling. That's powerful.

Stymied or Sent?

This leads me to my next point, the exception to the sending spoken of above. *"How shall they preach, except they be sent"* (Romans 10:15)? There is a biblical principle here that is undeniable, and that I agree with wholeheartedly. But there are exceptions, always; but they are the exceptions, not the rule. It may be sometimes a church lacks discernment, (of which there are very many in these days). Perhaps a man could be failed to be recognised and given the encouragement and support he ought to have because of church politics. Believe me, these things and worse happen in churches, and Reformed ones too. If you think not, hang around a bit. It could be because the minister is afraid of his position, or maybe he just does not like the man. All these things I have seen, do believe me. Maybe the man himself needs to be made aware of his gift and calling that is evident to all except him.

Then there may arise the issue of readiness. He is considered not ready yet. He needs at least two theological degrees and ten years to get them. I was reading a newspaper article a short while ago about a very talented soccer player. He was transferred to a very important team, never to be seen again for a long time. What had happened to this talent was the basis of this newspaper article. The answer given was they had over-coached him, ruined him. My point is you can go on and on learning (and you must), but never do anything with what you are learning. The theological course I took was started by Dr M. Lloyd-Jones, in South Wales. There was no certificate or degree at the finish. The idea was simply to produce preachers, that's all. I had already started preaching before commencing the course. All the faculty members insisted that the studies and the essays required must in no way hinder my preaching. That was the thing they wanted me doing more than anything else, preaching. If God's called you to preach that's what you should be doing. The coaching can be done in the background. Too much learning can make you useless on the street, maybe even turn you into a cerebral turkey, or a professional student, instead of a street preacher. You can quote Hebrew and Greek in a church building, but it won't get you anywhere on the street. Drug addicts, drunkards and other ne'er-do-wells normally don't understand English, never mind Hebrew and Greek. My own minister, church officers and the faculty members of the College were a great strength, encouragement and support to me. Alas, not all street preachers enjoy that same support, in fact very few. There are times a man has to do what a man has to do, as John Wayne once said. There are times when a man has to walk alone. A door must always remain open for men God has graciously qualified for service without special training.

That said, let it be noted, we do not and must not despise learning. If it is possible in the providence of God for a man to attend a good, sound seminary, then so be it. The main difficulty today would be finding such a seminary. But, that aside, we take note that the disciples sat at the feet of the Lord Jesus, being prepared for their ministry. The apostle Paul in God's providence sat at the feet of Gamaliel and had a very thorough training before he was called to his monumental task. There have been, and doubtless still are, many who despise and discount such preparation for ministry. Quakers and charismatics, Plymouth Brethren and Pentecostals, would be of such a mind. Good training for ministry is a good thing, but the best theological seminary in the world can never give a man what he needs for the ministry, i.e., godliness, modesty, common sense, and discretion. The ability to speak publicly, even eloquently, does not necessarily signify that a man should be a preacher of God's Word. But there will ever be men who God according to his good and sovereign pleasure, endows with gifts and abilities for the ministry, men who may not have been schooled in a seminary for many reasons, but have been supplied with gifts and abilities by God for ministry. The church is duty-bound to recognise and put such men to good use.

One thing that does need to be kept in mind is that before there were reformed pastors, there were street preachers, in Great Britain at least. If we go back to John Wycliffe's days, he contested then with the official clergy that they alone were not the church of God, but rather the congregation, the justified, those for whom Christ shed his blood. He held tenaciously to the free and immediate access of believers to the grace of God in Christ; to the general priesthood of all believers. It was as a result of this that like-minded believers gathered, and preachers were sent out from county to county and town to town, preaching, not just in churches, but also in churchyards, marketplaces and public thoroughfares. They contended with great emphasis that for the ministry of preaching, the Divine call and commission are perfectly sufficient; that the true installation of the preacher is that by God himself. I believe that heaven will testify of many who are there because of a wandering preacher who was never commissioned or laid hands on by men, but was most certainly called by God, and whose preaching God has owned in ways that this generation of preachers knows nothing of. I think it can be safely argued that without these fourteenth-century street preachers the Reformation of the sixteenth century would not have been possible. Wycliffe was persecuted, and some of the street preachers were burned, but the life created by this movement could not be extinguished.

So, I call upon despisers of street preachers to think again, modify your attitudes, and show some respect. One more thing, Dr M. Lloyd-Jones during his ministry strongly advocated that evangelism should be done solely by and through the local church.

I don't altogether disagree, but I think that he was taken far, far too literally. And the result has been twofold. One, where are all the back-street town and city Mission Halls and gospel ministries that used to feed the Reformed churches? They are no more. And two, sadly, evangelism is *not* being done by and through the local churches, not to the degree it ought and not to the extent it once was. This is a sadly sin-blighted land, where lawlessness increases by the day; religious apostasy abounds; the unrequited blood of unborn infants is shed; and there is explosion of a degraded and perverted human sexuality. The United Kingdom cries out for and provokes the judgment of the Almighty. How any Christian in their right mind can hinder in any way the gospel preaching of a sincere and serious godly brother in Christ defies reason.

Exhortation or Exposition?

The task of the preacher is to minister God's Word. There is a difference between exhorting and preaching. Sometimes an exhorter becomes a preacher. The gift of preaching is a charismatic gift sovereignly dispensed by the Holy Spirit as he wills. It is the ability to open up the Word of God, to explain its meaning clearly exposing to the minds of the hearers the divine counsel, and to challenge and apply that revealed truth also. I see and hear some men on the streets, and they are not preachers, expounders of God's Word, but exhorters exhorting people to believe the gospel. They speak about the gospel, Bible doctrines and so on, and they give reasons to people as to why they should believe the good news about Jesus Christ. This is fine as far as it goes, but it's not preaching. It is quite legitimate for a man to witness to his faith in such a way and people have doubtless come to faith through such exhortation. This exhorting was done a lot in Wales back in the days of revival. Men knew they were not preachers but they realised they could do something and so they would go out amongst the public exhorting people to believe and be saved.

And many did. But preaching is a God-given ability to break open the Word of God. The preacher doesn't simply give people random thoughts that come into his mind as to why his hearers ought to believe. The preacher takes a text of Scripture—it may be a phrase, a verse, or a portion of the Bible--and explains and applies it to those who will hear. But in terms of working on the street, it is different than from behind a pulpit desk, though the work is still the same. In a church situation the preacher has the time and leisure to read the Word of God and then, as he preaches, he will build up arguments and explain the minutia of his passage. No such leisure is given the street preacher, though he takes time to prepare just the same. He will find a short evangelistic or pithy phrase or verse of Scripture and he will open it up and apply it as he goes. But all he says is packed full of gospel truth because he may not have a static congregation. He may have someone for just a few minutes, but they will go away with saving truth nonetheless.

Let me give you an example (See Appendix 2). *"Christ died for the ungodly"* (Romans 5:6). It is short you see, and it summarises the gospel, and he can repeat it over and over, using it as a hammer to break the rock of sinful hearts. He expounds it as he goes along. What is the gospel? Number one: it's about a Person, Christ. Number two: what did he do? He died. Number three: Who for? The ungodly. You see there is order; he is not just giving people his random thoughts, what comes into his mind. It is the Word of God people's minds are being exposed to. And it is that alone which God has promised to use and bless, and nothing else, the faithful preaching of his Word.

Now a man may start as an exhorter. Perhaps that is all he can do, and he does his best. Well and good. But who knows, perhaps along the way God will bestow upon him the gift to preach. He can pray, as surely he must, and he can ask God for the gift to preach his Word. But do keep in mind that there is a difference between the two, exhortation and exposition. The next time you hear a street preacher, stop and listen, and ask yourself the question, 'What is he doing? Is he simply exhorting people, or is he expounding the text of Scripture?' Sadly I hear not a few men on the streets who ought not to be there exhorting even. This is one of the reasons that the task has a bad reputation. The price of freedom is that it's not always as tidy as we would like it to be. Alas, here lies the importance of a man being sent by his church, and this way it is not he who judges whether he has the God-given gift and ability to be on the street, either exhorting or preaching, but rather God's people, the church. Women are excluded from the public preaching ministry, not because men deserve this mantel. On the contrary, it is of grace, it is all of grace, from start to finish; but it has been given to men. We will return to this issue.

Evolution is a lie
Genesis 1:1

www.thestreetpreacher.co.uk

Jesus is Lord
Philippians 2:11

www.thestreetpreacher.co.uk

The Preacher's Voice

There was a day was when, if a man did not have a voice he would never have been a preacher. Today, with all kinds of electronic gadgets, weak-voiced men can and do get away with it. But, left without any such gadgets, how would *you* fair? Even some ministers and theologians in their churches and auditoriums would not be heard. It is one thing, believe me, to preach in a comfortable, warm, quiet, non-hostile environment and another in a cold, wet, hostile one, where mayhem is breaking out all around you. On the street, you need a voice. There are records of some of the renowned preachers of a former day, George Whitfield, for instance. It is said of Whitfield he could drop his voice to a whisper while preaching to thousands of people, and still be heard. Whitfield, of course, had planned a career on the stage before being converted and entering the ministry, so he would have learned how to use his voice to good effect. In the providence of God, this was a great blessing to him and the many who heard him. There have been others we could also mention. Preaching even in churches wasn't always as it is now. Today's ministers have it very easy. In Geneva, in John Calvin's day, the circumstances were somewhat different:

"Great preachers of the past such as Girolamo Savonarola in Florence and John Wesley in England may seem today bloodless on the printed page, for what most distinguished them is lost to us - their voice. Bland estimations of the Reformation speak of Protestantism as a religion of the book in contrast to the sensuous or affective religion of

the Middle Ages. To enter Calvin's world and the world of sixteenth-century Geneva requires imagination, a sense of how the spoken word could move, anger, console and edify. Far from the solemn quiet of modern churches, preaching in the sixteenth century was somewhat akin to speaking in a tavern. Preachers had to compete with barking dogs, crying babies, general chatter and constant movement, even fist-fights. They required presence to command respect and their most important tool was their voice. Johannes Oeclampadius, the reformer of Basle and a widely admired scholar, was rendered impotent in the pulpit by a weak voice. Written texts of Calvin's sermons exist, but they are problematic. They were recorded by others and provide only an inkling of what it must been like to hear to him. He spoke with no or few notes, and often with only a copy of the Bible in front of him; sheer spontaneity was an essential part of the experience as he applied God's Word to that moment in the life of the people. It was also a matter of time. With his endless pressing engagements, Calvin simply did not have the luxury of preparing sermons, so he spoke extempore. Nevertheless, when Calvin preached the people came" (Calvin, by B Gordon).

Today we get upset if the baby cries. Mum must take the child out or none will hear the preacher (even with his live microphone). If someone's mobile phone goes off, having forgotten to switch it off, ex-communication would be on the cards. But what if the person had the temerity to answer the phone call? Well, the description of Calvin's circumstances in Geneva does remind me of some the scenes I have encountered while preaching on the streets. How's your voice, young man? Do you have one? You'll need it. Oh, and if you're having trouble with your voice, sucking sweeties (candy) is not the answer–water is. Drink plenty of water.

Finally, to address Calvin's lack of time for preparation and his extempore preaching: the latter was not an excuse, or idleness. He was busy like we don't know how today. He was a man of great erudition. He studied, he was learned, indeed. This is not for someone to use as an excuse for not preparing himself for the Lord's service. On the subject of notes when preaching, it depends upon the individual. For some, having no notes at all would mean them endlessly repeating themselves, which some do. A small scrap of paper in one's Bible with a few words on it is not a crime. Alas, some ministers cry they have no time for preaching on the streets, they have books to read. So too, I'm sure, did John Calvin. But, study you must. Every city, town, village, and campus is different, and so too is each preaching opportunity. The preacher has to learn to adapt, and it is experience alone that will teach you this.

Again, Calvin, *"Comparisons of Calvin's sermons...reveals how the reformer adapted his language and style for the people while making few theological concessions. Accommodation did not mean dumbing down"* (Calvin, by B Gordon).

And again, *"The lot of the preacher and prophet was not only to be trained in sound doctrine but also so to be able to withstand attack and rejection. Calvin saw resistance as a sign of right preaching: a preacher must not avoid confrontation with the congregation; harsh words are often necessary"* (Calvin, by B Gordon).

Study and Submission

Today there are many helpful tools to help the young street preacher on the way into this ministry. You have many sermons on the internet, and volumes of written sermons that you would do well to study to see how men who have gone before you preached the gospel. You have also other street preachers who have posted their work on sites such as YouTube. Learn from them, the good, how to do it right; and the bad, from their mistakes, how not to do it. There is apologetic material available to help you deal with the many arguments against the gospel that people will raise. There is a series called *"Taking it to the Street"* by the late Dr Greg Bahnsen, excellent stuff. Jason Lisle and others write very helpfully, and you can find all these men and their material on the internet.

Then there are the many confessions of faith that we have at our disposal, including the works of the Westminster Assembly, their Confession, the Larger and Shorter Catechisms; The Belgic Confession of Faith, (written by Guido de Bres who was martyred for his confession of Christ in France); and The Canons of Dordt. Learning from the church of the past is vital, something that is seriously lacking in this generation. There is a huge and unjustifiable ignorance of these historical documents that have been passed on to us from former generations of godly men. Learn how the Calvinism versus Arminianism debate was dealt with, what is the history behind the arguments and the finer points? Go to the Canons of Dordt. Study and learn what it means to be Reformed and how to deal with the heresy of Arminianism. You want clarity on the much-disputed doctrine of justification by faith alone apart from works. Study the Westminster documents. Do you want material for preaching? The Shorter and Larger catechisms use questions and answers, such as, *"What is Sin?"*, *"What is Justification?"*, and *"What are the Punishments for sin in this Life?"* Take such questions to the street with you and answer them, clearly and with authority. And as you do so you will be teaching as well. The good man Luther said on one occasion, *"In preaching, I often find I'm preaching to myself."* We all do, so will you. We are never done learning. I've been at it for nearly forty years and I'm still learning. The more you learn the more assured you will be as to what the gospel is and isn't, and the more confident you will be to preach it.

There is no place in any church office or ministry for those who are ignorant of divine truth and who continue to remain so. This is even more important for anyone who is taking to the street with God's holy gospel. I have witnessed men attempting to preach on the streets who do not have a shred of doctrine in them, and by their performance, it is all too evident. The desire to minister is not the qualification. Just the other week I spoke with a young man here in my neighbourhood who told me he was out to proclaim the gospel. He said he had only weeks ago come to faith. His mentor, leader, or elder (I'm not sure what his ecclesiastical background was, neither was he) told him he was not ready for such a ministry. Whoever his leader was, he was perfectly correct. The young man was an ignoramus concerning biblical truth. It is such, of course, that gets street preaching a bad report, not to mention the damage such does to the general public. *"Lay hands suddenly on no man"* (1 Timothy 5:22).

Here lies the importance of a man having been sent by the authority of his local church, albeit the exceptions aside. Your fitness is for others to judge, not you. The man may have a tremendous testimony (doesn't every Christian?); the man may be likeable, affable, a friend, a family member, a good communicator, but all this is of no account. Has he shown himself to be faithful, teachable, and obedient in the context of his church situation? If not, will he be faithful to the truth outside the church? We hardly think so. I have seen men sent to seminaries or Bible colleges as candidates for ministry who have shown not an iota of spiritual gifting. The thinking is that the seminary or college will put it there. Wrong! It's God who puts it there. And if he hasn't put it there, nobody or anything else can or will. Are the words of Jesus appropriate here? *"If the blind lead the blind, both shall fall into the ditch"* (Matthew 15:14).

God requires not only decency amongst us but good order as well, *"Let all things be done decently and in order"* (1 Corinthians 14:40). If you neglect the spiritual policy that Christ teaches us in his Word, what does that say about you? Scripture says, therefore God says, *"Obey them that have the rule over you, and submit yourselves: for they watch for your souls, as they that must give account, that they may do it with joy, and not with grief: for that is unprofitable for you"* (Hebrews 13:17). In the West, there is amongst many in the church scene an Anabaptist culture (not necessarily to be equated with modern Baptists, more likened to modern-day extreme Pentecostalism). The Anabaptists were seditious people, who rejected the higher powers and magistrates, and ecclesiastical authority as well. They confounded the decency and good order that Scripture demands of us, and that also which God has established among men.

We are living in days when men enter into and set up ministries and churches without any ecclesiastical authority whatever. Some do so because they can't bear to be under submission themselves, and yet go on to expect others to yield to *their* authority. With such an attitude let no man venture on to the streets with God's holy Word. We are saved and sanctified *"unto obedience"* (1 Peter 1:2). The intended goal of Jesus Christ saving us is a life of obedience to God, and God's sanctifying work in us is to enable us to that end. The word 'decency' (1 Corinthians 14:40) means *"beautiful, honourable, and becoming."* Chaos and disorder are ugly as we see manifested in the society of the world. This is by no means to discourage. On the contrary, it is to save from such. Knowing first of all that you are qualified and equipped for the job before you start is better than finding out afterwards that you were not.

"For which of you, intending to build a tower, sitteth not down first, and counteth the cost, whether he have sufficient to finish it? Lest haply, after he hath laid the foundation, and is not able to finish it, all that behold it begin to mock" (Luke 14:28-29).

The Preacher's Bible

This is not a small issue. It is important that you not only have a good solid version of the Bible but that you've got it in your hand while you are preaching. With Bible in hand people know where you are coming from, that it is not your word, or your authority, but God's. In recent years there have been a plethora of versions produced. One can well imagine people being confused as to where God's Word is actually to be found, even Christians. With the plethora of versions produced in these modern times, the Word of God has been in effect taken away from the people. There are so many varying versions being used that a passage no longer sounds familiar. It has made memorisation of Scripture much harder as well. Also keep in mind that many of the modern versions have come to the fore in an age of modernism, apostasy, and doubt. That should be enough to cause us to suspect them. Many of them, such as the Living Bible, and the NIV, are not translations at all but paraphrases or partly so. Many will disagree with me, but the King James Version, or Authorised Version as it is sometimes called, is still by far the best. Its accuracy and faithfulness in the translation are superb— so much so that the English of the 1611 KJV is not the English of the 1600s as is sometimes stated, but rather it is *biblical English*, the result of the translators being as faithful as possible to the originals. It is not true that the modern versions are based on better manuscripts. That is a fallacy.

You will have to make up your mind in this matter. As the apostle says, *"Let every man be fully persuaded in his own mind"* (Romans 14:5). One thing is for sure, that when the street preacher lifts his voice and declares the Word of God using the King James Version, everybody knows where he is speaking from. Even the world's press organisations and theatricals, when they want to quote the Bible, what do they use? Uh-huh, the King James Version. That cannot be said of the modern versions. The King James Version of the Bible is not the only Bible, and there is much profit in consulting other versions, but I do believe it is still the best. Get yourself a proper Bible, preacher-man!

The Fear of Man

The subject of fear is addressed so much in Scripture that we can see that since the fall, it is a major issue. We fear every day, every single one of us. It is only lunatics who never fear. The antidote, of course, is faith in God, to fear him. *"Fear not them which kill the body, but are not able to kill the soul: but rather fear him which is able to destroy both soul and body in hell"* (Matthew 10:28).

But when it comes to the fear of man, that for the righteous is a sinful fear, and to be repented of. The prophet Isaiah, says, *"Hearken* unto me, ye that know righteousness, the people in whose heart is my law; fear ye not the reproach of men, neither be ye afraid of their revilings" (Isaiah 51:7).

If you know righteousness, the righteousness of God that is, and that you are righteous by faith in Jesus Christ, what do you have to fear from men? It is this fear of man that keeps Christians from confessing the Lord before men. We have all been guilty of it many times. But it has no place in the street preacher's or any Christian's heart.

I was ministering with a man in the United States a short while ago, who works for Trans World Radio. I asked him about any feedback they got from their broadcasts into Middle Eastern countries. He told of people who listened to the broadcasts in bathrooms and cupboards for fear of detection, but others who asked for prayer because they had come to the place where they could no longer keep their faith secret. They felt constrained to confess their Lord before others, but knew it would mean certain death for them. By the grace of God through faith in Christ, our fear can and must be overcome. I have said it often enough, but I say it again, courage is not the absence of fear, but is doing and saying what is right in spite of the presence of that fear. The bolder you confess his name the more boldness will be given to you. But rest assured you will excite hostility and bring many reproaches upon yourself as you declare Christ among the lost. You will be taunted and insulted. Read the book of Jeremiah if you will. See what that righteous man had to endure. But the Lord told him he would make him like a bronze wall. They blaspheme against God. But look at what Isaiah says of those who reproach and revile you for His sake: *"Fear not… for the moth shall eat them up like a garment, and the worm shall eat them like wool"* (Isaiah 51:8). That's the end of those who revile your testimony, and the preaching of the Word of God. Soon they will be no more, the grave will consume them, and hell shall be their destruction unless they repent. But the gospel you proclaim will go on conquering and will conquer to the end. *"But my righteousness shall be for ever, and my salvation from generation to generation"* (Isaiah 51:8b).

The prophet writes under the inspiration of God to strengthen his people, to embolden them. Do not let the insults, the reviling of men, deter you. God has the back of his people when they are abused. *"For ye have not received the spirit of bondage again to fear"* (Romans 8:15). Read again the heroes of the faith in Hebrews chapter eleven. Many have gone before us who counted not their lives dear unto them, but were, *"rejoicing that they were counted worthy to suffer shame for his name"* (Acts 5:41). The fear of man is sinful and must be repented of, and grace sought to overcome by the blood of the Lamb.

> When I'm afraid I'll trust in thee:
> In God I'll praise his Word;
> I will not fear what flesh can do,
> my trust is in the Lord.
>
> In God his Word I'll praise; his Word
> in God shall praised be.
> In God I trust; I will not fear
> what man can do to me?
>
> *(Scottish Psalter 56:3-4, 10-11).*

Evolution is a lie
Genesis 1:1
Jesus is Lord
Philippians 2:11
www.thestreetpreacher.co.uk
After
you die,
you will
meet God
Repent of your sin
before it's too late,
and believe on the
Lord Jesus Christ!
www.thestreetpreacher.co.uk

Preaching or Performance?

Some men think that they have to use 'stage effects' or have a 'stage presence' to present the gospel. It will most likely get you a crowd, even get you a following, but it will be for the wrong reasons. Many were not content with the apostle Paul's preaching. They thought that he lacked oratory, rhetorical skills. In other words, he didn't have the charisma, the 'stage presence' (2 Corinthians 10:10; 1 Corinthians 1:17, 2:1, 4). His speech was *'rude,'* they said (2 Corinthians 11:6). The word translated as rude here (ιδιωτης) means unskilled, uneducated, or unlearned, an idiot in other words. They thought that he was a man unskilled in the art form of rhetoric. It's not the message, the content, that's the issue, but Paul's preaching. No theatrics, no bodily movement: he just speaks. He has no charisma. A dictionary meaning of the word charisma is: *"a personal magic of leadership arousing special popular loyalty or enthusiasm for a public figure, due to his charisma."*

Take it from me, you can do without the magic, and so could Paul. And he erected a New Testament church. Paul simply and clearly preached the gospel, lest it should be robbed of its power; lest men's faith should come to rest in him and his gifts rather than in the power of God (1 Corinthians 2:1-4). That's exactly what happens when men turn the act of preaching into theatrics, into a performance. The Word of God is what the Holy Spirit uses, and nothing else, to bring men to faith in Jesus Christ-- not the antics, not the theatrics, not the rhetoric, not the oratory gifts of men.

Genuine conversion is produced by a renewing of the mind of man through the application of God's Word by the Holy Spirit (Romans 12:2; Ephesians 4:21-23; 2 Timothy 1:17). Your performance may get you a crowd but it may also get you false converts. Is this God's call for you? Is this God's intent for his kingdom? Paul rails against such practice, for God has chosen to do things differently from the world and its theatrics. He does not call silver-tongued speakers, smooth operators or demagogues with their inflated ideas of their gifting and personalities—and why? *"That no flesh should glory in his presence"* (1 Corinthians 1:29).

This has been and still is a major problem in the church. A couple of examples: Dr M Lloyd-Jones here in the United Kingdom, Christian, Reformed, and Calvinistic in his theology, with a faithful ministry over many years. He prioritised *'style'* as an essential in preaching. He championed rhetorical oratory, a performance in the pulpit, preaching as *'an art form'*. (See his "Preaching and Preachers"). Jesus and his apostle, Paul, often sat down to preach, so they would not have used their whole bodies as Lloyd-Jones advocated. Of course, the man gained large audiences: he became an idol of the Reformed fraternity. I do not say he looked for that, but he got it. For many years after his departure from this life, we heard the words over and again, "The Doctor said," the implication being if he said it then it must be right. Men are followed and idolised in the church today in like fashion, I could name one or two, but I won't.

Another from the past though, Robert Murray M'Cheyne, who himself recognised that there was a problem. So many attended church to hear *him* not God's Word. People were attracted to him, doted on him, not Christ. Many who came to hear him never became believers. This all came out in his pastoral work, and it troubled him. Of course, he didn't want this. It grieved him, it pained him, but it happened. I often think of our evangelical hero, George Whitfield, who himself was theatre-bound before his conversion. It has been more than once suggested that his dramatic performances had more to do with the crowds than the gospel (see 'The Divine Dramatist' by H.R Stout).

My point is, God does not need your rhetorical, theatrical skills. Beware and be done with theatrics. Just preach the gospel. Paul went to Corinth in weakness and in trembling. His power was in the message, the gospel, the content, what he preached, not his preaching *style,* for he had none. God's Word by the power of God's Spirit will accomplish God's will. Your place is simply to convey that Word to men and women, simply, plainly, without any theatrics at all. If you want to perform, leave the pulpit and go to Hollywood. They will welcome you there.

Winning Some or Winsome

As the holy Gospel is the true treasure entrusted to God's people (2 Corinthians 4:7), so the preaching of that gospel is the primary task of the church and her preachers. The well-worn saying amongst the Arminian fraternity used to be and probably still is, *"You have to be winsome to win some."* In other words, you have to be a friendly, sociable kind of preacher. The Hebrew word for *preaching* means to be fresh, then cheerful, then to tell good tidings. According to classical Greek, this person was a herald, a public crier, a messenger vested with authority who conveyed the official message of kings, magistrates, princes, and military commanders. In his lexicon, Mayer adds that the *manner* of a herald was *"always with a suggestion of formality, gravity, and an authority which must be listened to and obeyed."* In other words, you must bear a commanding presence amongst the public you are addressing. This is the word the New Testament writers were inspired to use for preachers and the activity of preaching. A preacher is God's ambassador, or official messenger, who conveys the Word of God to others. This is most beautifully and clearly stated in 2 Corinthians 5:20: *"We are therefore Christ's ambassadors, as though God were making his appeal through us. We implore you on Christ's behalf: be reconciled to God"*.

Preaching is the chief means of grace, for by it the Holy Spirit implants faith. Preaching is one of the marks by which the true church may be easily distinguished from the false. Preaching, with very few exceptions, is necessary for salvation! Debating is not the means that God has ordained for the salvation of the elect, but the preaching of the Word is that means. This is shown clearly in Romans 10, where faith and salvation is shown to come as a result of hearing, through preaching, but firstly by the sending of the preacher (v14). The simple conclusion, is, *"So then faith cometh by hearing, and hearing by the word of God"* (v17). The preaching of the cross is said to be the power of God for salvation, no matter how foolish such preaching appears to some. It is for this reason the apostle is not ashamed of the gospel of Christ, for it is the power of God for salvation to everyone who believes (Romans 1:16). It is not your winsomeness that will save, but the preaching of God's Word.

Oh, you will be asked time and again by fellow believers, "Is this the best way to do this?" They will suggest that it would be better to befriend people and gradually and winsomely introduce them to the gospel, but only when they are ready. The trouble is in the meantime they may perish, so such an attitude lacks the urgency of the matter. But apart from that, the calling is not to befriend people but to preach the gospel. And they may never be ready. It will be suggested that by your authoritative approach and perceived lack of winsomeness you will push people further away from God. Can a sinner under sin and the wrath of God by nature and practice, existing daily on the edge of everlasting torments be any further away from God than that, I ask you? I am not suggesting you be anything less than joyful as you go about the Master's business and most certainly we must not appear to be anti-social. But it is a serious, a solemn business: *"He that heareth you heareth me; and he that despiseth you despiseth me; and he that despiseth me despiseth him that sent me"* (Luke 10:16).

In the West today there is a famine *"of hearing the words of the LORD"* (Amos 8:11). What could be more dreadful, more serious than that, for then Christ does not speak through the preacher? These are not days for the foolish notions of men, but serious, strong proclamation. In all true preaching, Christ is central. Christ speaks;

Christ is the content of the message, as faith in Him crucified and raised is commanded. Christ, by His Spirit, makes the preaching effectual so that those ordained to eternal life believe. More important than being winsome is that you are faithful in the preaching of the Word of God. If you have the desire, the call of God, and the gift to preach God's Word, what a blessing! What beautiful feet you have! *"How beautiful are the feet of them that preach the gospel of peace, and bring glad tidings of good"* (Romans 10:15)! This is much more important than winsomeness.

Preaching is Man's Work

I happened upon a video clip of a young woman preaching on the street in England a short while ago. It greatly saddened me. She did not have the knowledge or understanding of the gospel, which was clear by what she said. Also, she did not have a voice for public speaking, let alone preaching. There was not an iota of authority in what she was presenting. In short, it was appallingly pathetic. But worse still it was an act of disobedience to God. I wrote to her gently, remonstrating with her, but to no avail. I have witnessed another more elderly woman here locally preaching also. Then there is Angela from the USA. She most certainly has a voice and speaks with some authority—but not God's authority. Why? Because ministers must be men: the Bible says so. It is bad enough that in the present generation we could say that many of our men are insufficiently masculine, but calling women to the ministry is not an answer to that problem.

Ask yourself the question, "Why did Jesus not include women in his apostolate?" I mean, we're in the new covenant era, so if a break with the old patriarchal system was to be made, that would have been the time, yes? To have included women in the preaching ministry wouldn't have rocked any boats as far as the world was concerned. It wouldn't have raised an eyebrow. Paganism was infested with priestesses, but the church went against the grain. It took the unpopular route. Some would and do argue it would be a great help in reaching other womenfolk. Yet God refrains them from the preaching ministry (1 Timothy 2:8-15). A woman is not allowed to vote in a congregational meeting, *"I suffer not a woman to teach, nor to usurp authority over the man"* (1 Timothy 2:12). It's not that what Paul says is unclear, it's just simply inconvenient to this generation, it seems. But obedience is obedience, is it not? And faithfulness is faithfulness, is it not?—to Scripture I mean.

Paul even gives reasons. 1) The order of creation (v13). 2) The woman, not Adam, was first deceived (v14). Then, she *taught* Adam in the garden. She usurped authority over him (Genesis 3:6), so the reason a woman is excluded from the preaching ministry is not because of first-century cultural mores. It goes back to creation and the fall. The person who says, "That was then, in Paul's day," gets it wrong. Paul's inspired and infallible reasoning goes back beyond even his day, back six thousand years. There is a divine order (1 Corinthians 11:3-10). For women to teach and preach and to rule over men is unhealthy. The first time it happened it was catastrophic, the fall. Much more could be said about this, but enough for now.

In the public arena, in the market square or street corner, we have a mixed multitude, men as well as women. It is plainly and simply a matter of obedience or not. We live in a generation, in the West anyway, where people are reinventing themselves, their gender, sexuality. Men and women now are interchangeable. There is cultural chaos, in and out of the church. Does this mean that women have no part to play in evangelistic work? Not at all. I know of many ladies who accompany the menfolk, some their husbands, on the streets. They pray, they distribute literature, and they engage people in conversation. Some have proved themselves to be excellent helpers. A lady in my church in Glasgow is in her eighties. Her husband is a retired minister. The flat where they live overlooks the entrance to Glasgow University. She often stands at that entrance giving out tracts and gospels to all who will have them. You see, we can do *something*—but if ever we needed the preaching men that the Reformed faith once upon a time produced it is now, men who are serious, stern, biblically rigorous, and full of the Holy Ghost. It is now. *"Quit you like men"* (1 Corinthians 16:13).

Christ & Him Crucified

There are only two classes of people in this world from God's perspective, the saved and the perishing. And there is but only one means God has appointed to save the perishing—the preaching of the cross of his Son Jesus Christ. It was while I was at the above-mentioned college that one of the faculty members asked our class one day how we saw our calling to preach. He went around the class one by one. They all without exception, like parrots, said, "To teach the flock and build up the saints." It didn't go very far when the said professor stopped them, *"Wrong",* he said, "You are all wrong!" "The salvation of souls! That is what should be at the front of your minds every time that you preach." *"Every sermon ought to be evangelistic"* (Dr M. Lloyd-Jones). You can do no greater hurt to your hearers than to allow the cowardly or despisers of the cross to deflect you from this. The calling is not to please men, win their applause, to please their ears or sing them a song. You are called to save men's perishing souls. If you are not convinced that men are dead, not a little bit, but dead in their sins; and if you are not convinced to the depth of your being that the only way these perishing sinners can be made alive is by the Holy Spirit empowered, God-ordained means, the preaching of the cross, you will never convert a flea. In a word, you must preach Christ. You must be convinced in your mind that preaching alone is God's ordained method (1 Corinthians 1:22). Question 155 of the Westminster Larger Catechism asks, *"How is the Word made effectual to salvation? A. The Spirit of God maketh the reading, but especially the preaching of the Word, an effectual means of enlightening, convincing, and humbling sinners; of driving them out of themselves, and drawing them unto Christ; of conforming them to his image, and subduing them to his will."*

The calling is not to engage in social work, but to preach—in university campuses, in the marketplace, wherever men are gathered—to preach and to preach Christ. There are those in religious, and yes, even Christian circles today who disdain preaching very much. At best they think it to be a secondary, even irrelevant, activity. The liberals, the snowflakes, you will encounter them all. They will tell you of the world's needs, the earthquake zones, the starving, the storm lashed regions where the needs are so great. "You should be helping those people," they will tell you, "Not preaching." No, preaching is the church's and the street preacher's primary task. It is preaching that saves men's souls from eternal damnation, something much worse than any storm, earthquake or disaster imaginable. It is preaching that brings new and everlasting life to men's souls, nothing else. If you are not convinced of that, do not begin until you are.

Law and the Gospel

When we speak of preaching Christ or the gospel, or preaching the cross, we are not speaking about simply and only preaching from the New Testament or from those particular phrases. To preach Christ is to preach the whole counsel of God because the whole Bible is the word of Christ, so to neglect preaching the law and the prophets would be a serious mistake; especially so the law, *"for by the law is the knowledge of sin"* (Romans 3:20). How does a person come to know that they need a Saviour without first coming to know that they have a condition that they need saving from, a sin problem? That is the purpose of the Divine law, summarised in the Ten Commandments. The Ten Commandments themselves are a wonderful preaching tool for the street preacher. You must preach on them regularly. The law is a teacher, a schoolmaster (Galatians 3:24), to teach men how holy God is and how sinful they are. The purpose of the law is to shred man's self-righteousness and to send him to Christ to be saved. *"For Christ is the end of the law for righteousness to every one that believeth"* (Romans 10:4). That does not mean that Christ is the end of the law to take it away, but rather that he is the end of the law by being its goal, its purpose. The law was given with Christ in mind, by uncovering sin, showing men their need of Christ and of being justified through faith in him. The law continues to function this way to this day, *"I had not known sin, but by the law"* (Romans 7:7), says the apostle, Paul. The law is a schoolmaster not just for the Jews, but for us too. The law is part of the covenant of grace (Galatians 3:19). It still belongs to the covenant. Law and grace are not against each other. It is also a sure and safe guide along the pilgrim's pathway (Psalm 119:105; Proverbs 6:23), but we must understand that the law does not bring man into a covenant relationship with God, nor does is give us grace, justify us. This he gets from Christ and Christ alone. The law (Moses) tells the broken sinner to go to Christ and live.

The Preacher's Apologetic

To be armed with a good, solid defense of the Christian faith is essential on the street. The arguments will come thick and fast. There will be atheists, philosophers and the false religions to deal with. The question is, where do you go, and how can you be best equipped to deal with such. There are, according to the Oxford University Press, nine thousand nine hundred religions in the world today, and not one of them has an ounce of saving power and grace. Christianity is not a religion. It is a life and worldview. I have already mentioned one or two sources for help, but let me mention them again. There are two systems, if you like, of apologetic. There is the *Classical* and there is the *Presuppositional*. I tend to favour the latter but there is not much between them, to be honest. Sources? The late Dr Greg Bahnsen's excellent book *"Always Ready."* is a *must-read* for any would-be street preacher. Bahnsen also has a series of DVD's still available called *"Taking in the Streets"*—all very useful stuff.

However, that's not the place to begin. The starting place is a thorough study of Romans chapter one, especially verses sixteen to the end. You cannot overdo your attention to this portion of Scripture. That is your apologetic before anything and anyone else. All of these early chapters of Romans are vital to show the actual state of man's condition in sin, which in turn brings you to see that without the sovereign almighty grace of God he has no hope at all. It is for that reason Paul says he is *"ready"* (v15) to preach the gospel. He makes it clear that men, all men, are not devoid of the knowledge of

God. They know that God is the same way the preacher knows. They have an innate knowledge of God. But that knowledge is *"held"* (v18), held down that is, suppressed in unrighteousness.

One of Bahnsen's illustrations serves to make the point. Daddy takes the kids to the beach, and out comes the beach ball. Daddy takes the ball into the water and sits on it, pressing it down under the water. He calls out to the kids, "Where's the ball?" Of course, the kids know fine and well where the ball is. Daddy is playing the fool. He too knows where the ball is. He is suppressing it, holding it down under the water—but he needs some power to do that. He holds it under with all his strength. Why? Because the ball wants to keep pushing back up. That is a man without God. He holds down the knowledge of God with all his God-given powers and talents—anything but let it surface. But the street preacher knows he is playing the fool (Psalm 14:1). Many things keep forcing that truth up—creation, providence, his conscience—so he has to fight to keep the truth of the knowledge of God down. He'll use Darwin, Dawkins, false science, philosophic ideas, anything he can get his hands on to justify his unbelief, but he is doing it unrighteously, sinfully, wickedly, He needs to repent and believe the gospel, the only way back to God and forgiveness. It is because of God's operations in creation and providence that he, whoever he is, is without excuse, without an apologetic, a defense, for his unbelief (v20).

As a result of his departure, rejection of God, that God has given him up (v24). Man says he doesn't want God, his Son, his salvation, his love, so God says in effect: "Okay, as you don't want me, I will open another door, and I'll even help you through the door. I will give you over to another power, to the power of self. God gives men what they want. It is the worst judgment that can fall upon a person in all this world, to be given over to the power of self, to do what we naturally desire, sin. Hence, God punishes sin with more and more sin (vv24-32). It's dreadful, awful. And it's why we need to be preaching the gospel because that is the only remedy. But it is imperative that you know your Bible, that you study Romans chapter one, and that you study apologetics, the defense of the Christian faith.

> Evolution is a lie,
> Some people ask me, why;
> Science, science is what I hear them cry,
> But even this they do, not knowing why.
> Science's good, a conceptual tool,
> But not for the truth an absolute rule;
> Your reasoning can be wrong, even fail,
> Lead you down to the depths of hell.
>
> Truth is eternal, it has always been,
> And it doesn't come because of what you've seen;
> Senses are good but upon them you must not lean,
> For truth, on theories, devised by men.
> Info is good but is never found in a lump of matter,
> But in an intelligent mind, in God the Creator;
> From the mind of a person a glorious Saviour,
> The only source of such a wonderful treasure.
>
> Laws abound, of nature, logic and love,
> Surely all such's from heaven above;
> From the mind of God revealed in love,
> So we could rule, and for his glory live.
> So evolution is a lie,
> Upon it, you must not rely;
> Or in sin, you will die,
> God's Word is the truth, it's on that, you must rely.
>
> (© Jimmy Hamilton aka The Street Preacher, 24th June 2017)

However, in studying apologetics, the danger is that we can get side-tracked; that apologetics becomes the be-all and end-all.

You learn how to fight your corner, argue your case (graciously, of course). You learn to win and to enjoy winning arguments. That's not what you're on the street for. You are there to preach the gospel. Never forget that! You are not there to debate, or to argue, and you are not there to preach apologetics. Your apologetic is the means of removing the smoke from the room so that Christ can be preached. In the course of preaching you use the apologetic method, but always with the desire to get to real issues: sin, salvation, and Christ. I've listened to men spend an hour preaching, fifty-five minutes of which is spent on apologetics, and the gospel is tagged on at the end, in the last five minutes. That will not do. You are there to preach Jesus Christ and him crucified for sinners. You can win arguments, but that is not winning souls. *"He that winneth souls is wise"* (Proverbs 11:30).

Fruit & Faithfulness

The question will be asked of you sooner or later, "What fruit have you seen in this ministry?" Or they may ask, "Is this the best way of doing this? Why don't you just tell them that God loves them?" They will tell you, "You need to build friendships with them," "You shouldn't judge people," and so on. It goes on, and on, and on. I was once asked by a young lady, while I was preaching, why I was doing what I was doing. I thought that that was obvious, but not to her. "We don't do this," was her reply, "We give them doughnuts, and we do treasure hunts." Yes, she was serious. She was her church's mission leader even. This is what we've come to, liberalism in the church gone viral.

So how do you gauge your effectiveness, fruitfulness, in terms of your calling? That's not as easy, or as black and white as some would perhaps assume it to be. Souls saved, professions of faith made? If someone were to tell me tomorrow that they had professed faith in Christ as a result of my preaching yesterday, I would be happy, encouraged, but not too much. If someone were to tell me tomorrow that they had come to faith as a result of my preaching ten years ago, and that they are still trusting and serving the Lord, then I would be rejoicing, jumping up and down with the angels in heaven. But if your ministry is peripatetic, i.e., a travelling preacher— and there is room for such a calling in the New Testament church (Trust me on this: you will never be loved and accepted by the Reformed church as such until God removes the blindness from their eyes to see it)

—then mostly you will be sowing seed. You may return after many days and find it has borne some fruit. You might not. There are times when God lifts the curtain and gives us a peek behind the scenes to see what he is doing, for our encouragement. But rest assured you're in this for the long haul, and it can be a long, long, hard road, with many disappointments and hardships along the way. The young prophet Jeremiah preached for some thirty years and never saw a convert. You must keep on, even if none believe.

The prophet Isaiah was called in a time of appalling declension in Israel, but his ministry was fruitful. The fruit?—utter devastation and dereliction, with the nation ending up in exile (Isaiah 6:9ff). The people were to hear and see, though they would not understand or perceive (Isaiah 6:9), and he was to lift his voice, crying aloud against their transgressions (Isaiah 58:1). It was to be a message of sin, warning, and judgment to come. That was not an easy, comfortable commission, and you're not going to change your nation or the world either. The prophet's preaching, God assured him, would harden the majority by the operations of his wrath. That's what you are faced with in Western society today. The message is not one of grace and love for all. But the Word is to be preached promiscuously, to all who will hear, whatever their response may be. And for many, the more they understand you the more they will set all their God-given powers against the Almighty and his Son Jesus Christ, just like old Pharaoh, *"Who is the Lord that I should serve him?"* Of course, it didn't deter Isaiah, but then he was called. Does this put you off, discourage you? Then maybe you're not called? I'm just being realistic. You need to know what you're getting into before you begin. In every generation, everywhere, God has his remnant, his chosen, his elect, and we comfort ourselves in this, that they will be saved. I do not have to drive myself into the ground seeking to produce fruit. I have only to be faithful to my calling and God's precious Word.

I was encouraged by an elderly man many years ago. He related this to me. A youngster, sixteen years of age, was invited by a friend's family to a gospel service in England. This preacher expounded the text, *"If any man loves not the Lord Jesus Christ, let him be accursed"* (1 Corinthians 16:22). The youngster left that service unmoved, untouched. He moved with his family to Canada sometime later, enjoyed a successful farming career, and a good number of years' retirement. In his early eighties, the Holy Spirit in mighty power brought that text back to him in saving power in his living room, breaking, convicting and converting him. The point is, you might not see the fruit of your ministry in this life. You're called to be faithful, that's all.

There's always a difficulty in bringing the model of the Great Awakening to our situation. They had revival, while we are faced with decline, so the *success* rate needs to be seriously tempered. This work has always been, and I think always will, be difficult. Churches, presbyteries and ministers love to eulogise George Whitfield and the Wesley's very much, and quote them abundantly; but if you dare to seek to emulate those whom they love to eulogise they will not want to know you (they only love the dead ones). Or, perhaps, if you strike gold, God sovereignly granting you a vein of gospel success (success, that is, in their terms) then they will excuse you, love you, embrace you and even give you a warm smile. They may even open their pulpits. Then you will be the best thing since sliced bread. But until then we will continue to be the extremists, the Cinderella's of the church. That's another reason I tell young men who have an inclination to preach on the streets that they must be prepared to stand alone against all comers, sometimes sadly, very sadly, even the churches. If you can't do that, then don't even begin.

Keep Swinging the Bat

Let me assume that you have been sent: you are an ambassador with the King's authority to deliver his message. You have the Divine promise that Christ will speak through you. If he doesn't speak through the preaching, all that is heard is the sound of a man's voice and is of no avail. We live in times in the West when preaching is thought to have failed if it hasn't filled the church or if the preacher doesn't have many scalps under his belt. The Lord knows how we have all felt the weight of failure in our preaching. And we have all had those times when we vowed to never to preach again. There has never been a preacher born of a woman who has not ever felt that way, except perhaps the Lord Jesus Christ himself. No, you're not alone. We have all been there before you and we have got the T-shirt as well. But just like us, you will go back and back and back again and do it again, if God has called you. You just keep swinging the bat. But if you are to persevere in the preaching it is imperative to understand what the divine purpose, God's intent, is in the preaching of his Word.

The Intent in the Preaching of God's Word

What is God's intention in this great calling? It is to establish his covenant, that is, to gather, redeem, deliver, and free his elect. For this, he has entrusted us with his Word, holy Scripture. The Words were divinely conceived and have God as their content: it's a self-revelation. It is his given Word alone that we have authority to proclaim. Objectively, he has given us the Bible and he has preserved it as promised. Subjectively, he, by his Spirit has given us his Word in our hearts (John 16:13-14). He, the Holy Spirit, is the Author of the Word and uses nothing else in the fulfilling of God's purpose. His ultimate aim is a new heaven and new earth in which will dwell his elect. But to get there the very last of God's children must be called, justified, and sanctified. The entire body of Christ has to be filled up, and this by the preaching of God's Word. We like to speak of this saving effect of the Word, but it is only one side of the coin, so to speak.

The ungodly world must be disinherited and fitted for destruction.

For this to be fulfilled the world needs to be ripened for judgment and condemnation. Only then, faced with the perfect righteous judgement of God, can the reprobate be eternally destroyed. What is the connection? The preaching of God's Word also accomplishes this. The preaching of the gospel, your preaching, is a two-edged sword: *""For we are unto God a sweet savour of Christ, in them that are saved, and in them that perish: To the one we are the savour of death unto death; and to the other the savour of life unto life. And who is sufficient for these things?"* (2 Corinthians 2:15-16). *"Therefore hath he mercy on whom he will have mercy, and whom he will he hardeneth"* (Romans 9:18). One is ripened for salvation the other for damnation. God has promised to use his Word to this end. But only the Word of God can accomplish it, nothing else. His Word always accomplishes his will, whatever that Divine will may be: *"So shall my word be that goeth forth out of my mouth: it shall not return unto me void, but it shall accomplish that which I please, and it shall prosper in the thing whereto I sent it"* (Isaiah 55:11).

The Importance of the Faithful Preaching of God's Word

It is the faithful, honest preaching of God's Word that will bring you all manner of strife. It is a very dangerous and hard road that you will travel upon. It is not for men-pleasers, for dandy's or snowflakes. It cost John the Baptist his head: *"And when the messengers of John were departed, he began to speak unto the people concerning John, What went ye out into the wilderness for to see? A reed shaken with the wind? But what went ye out for to see? A man clothed in soft raiment? Behold, they which are gorgeously apparelled, and live delicately, are in kings' courts. But what went ye out for to see? A prophet? Yea, I say unto you, and much more than a prophet"* (Luke 7:24-26). You will incur the wrath of men and devils. You will be reproached, reviled, and made to suffer. You will be persecuted, and maybe even face death. The faithful preaching of the Word will maybe get you souls, but it will surely get you enemies, both in and out of churches. The world lies in wickedness (1 John 5:19). It is of the devil, and they will do his will. The world hates what you stand for and what you preach. Do not be surprised at this. It is normal—if, that is, you remain faithful to the Word of God.

When you incur such hatred of men you must remember what it did to Christ, your Master, and to his apostles. Why? Because they were faithful in preaching God's Word. Read about the heroes of the faith in Hebrews 11. Read your church history, the Waldensians, the Scottish Covenanters, and Foxe's Book of Martyrs. Faithful men and women were slain, and their blood cries out from under the altar for vindication: *"And they cried with a loud voice, saying, How long, O Lord, holy and true, dost thou not judge and avenge our blood on them that dwell on the earth?"* (Revelation 6:9).

Of course, you can take the pressure off. You can tamper with and twist the Word of God, or you can outright deny the Word of God. The world will agree with you, love you. But if you are faithful in preaching God's literal six-day creation; if you preach against sin; if you clearly define God's institution of marriage; and preach the sovereign grace of God that saves apart from works of any kind, they will hate you, vilify you, and curse you. But God's hand of protection will be upon you. At worst they may kill you and send you to heaven, but no more: *"Fear not them which kill the body, but are not able to kill the soul: but rather fear him which is able to destroy both soul and body in hell"* (Matthew 10:28).

May God bless his preachers of righteousness and keep them bold and strong in the power of his might, and may his sovereign and ultimate purpose be soon fulfilled. Men! Keep swinging the bat. *"Surely I come quickly. Amen. Even so, come, Lord Jesus"* (Revelation 22:20).

Preaching the Judgment of God

The famous sermon of Jonathan Edwards, *"Sinners in the Hands of an Angry God,"* is well known to most men in the preaching fraternity. I read that Edwards did not preach that sermon howling like a banshee. On the contrary, he preached it in a fairly quiet and mild manner. It was the force and intensity of the Word that brought about the result of people holding on to the pillars of the church fearing they would drop into hell. That was the work and power of the Holy Ghost. But we live in different days. Those old-time preachers were bulletproof. They could almost call down the flames of hell until people could nigh on smell the sulphur, feel the heat. But that fear of hell is almost gone, in Western society at least anyway. Now most preachers don't even mention it anymore. Actually, most don't preach anymore, they just give talks. To be termed a 'hell-fire preacher' today is not a respectable accolade, so few men preach fear, and the pulpit has become anæmic in its preaching about punishment.

Yet the entire cosmos groans under the curse of God because of man's apostasy, *"For we know that the whole creation groaneth and travaileth in pain together until now"* (Romans 8:22). We have the clear and distinct evidence of the Almighty's wrath, *"For the wrath of God is revealed from heaven against all ungodliness and unrighteousness of men, who hold who hold the truth in unrighteousness"* (Romans 1:18). It is all over us like a rash, but sinners are both deaf and blind to it. They need to be awakened out of their sleep of death. They need to hear about their involvement in sin *and* its consequences, both temporal and eternal—so we use fear, wholesome fear. You will never fetch a sinner to the cross by telling jokes, or by making casual remarks about their sin. I even heard a preacher, a team-leader, a short while back, blaspheme God's name! "Oh," said he with a smile, "Sorry about the mistake." A mistake? Sin! Blasphemy! There is a world to come, *"Behold, the judge standeth before the door"* (James 5:9). To give a pleasant gospel talk may make you popular and get you a return visit, but it will leave your hearers, the world, untouched, unregenerate, unsaved.

Sin is man's 'no' to God. Wrath is God's 'no' to man's sin. One day men will be nothing but objects of that wrath for all eternity, except they repent and believe the gospel (Mark 1:15). Jesus said very clear and awful things regarding the unrepentant. The word hell is itself terrifying. The word has all but been banished from the modern translations of the Bible. Without the preaching of hell, the command of the gospel loses its urgency. *"And fear not them which kill the body, but are not able to kill the soul: but rather fear him which is able to destroy both soul and body in hell"* (Matthew 10:28). Am I saying we need to frighten people into being saved? No. But often it is the fear of judgment, the doctrine of eternal punishment that God uses to save his people. It is an important part of gospel preaching, and not yours to exclude from your preaching.

Some we will drive with fear and others we will draw with love into the arms of Jesus. We may preach the certainty of the coming judgment, but we must not forget also to preach the love God evidenced in the death of his only begotten Son; for he sent his Son for this reason: *"Whom God hath set forth to be a propitiation through faith in his blood, to declare his righteousness for the remission of sins that are past, through the forbearance of God"* (Romans 5:25)—that is, to deal with his very own wrath, that in divine love and mercy it might be removed from us.

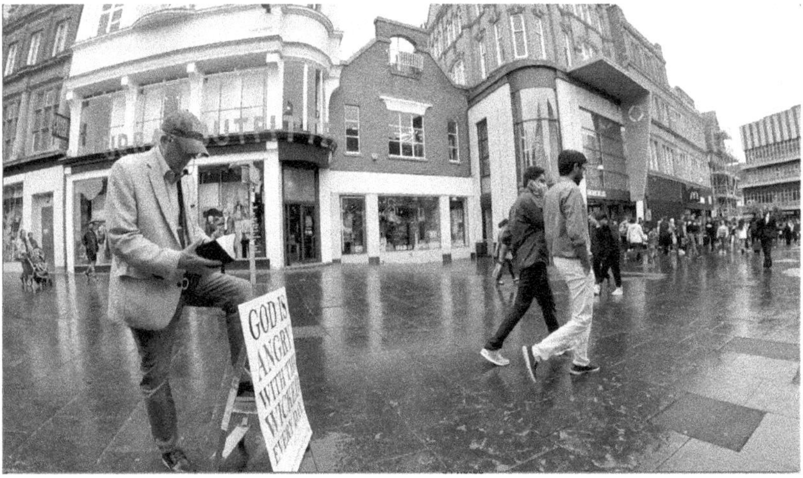
GOD IS
ANGRY

Preaching with Passion

I was preaching with some other men in a town close by some years ago. A man stopped briefly to listen to the one who was preaching at the time. Another colleague asked him, "Do you believe what he is preaching?" "No," said the man, "but he does." A man on fire! The Holy Ghost needs to burn the message into your heart before others will feel the heat. There is the well-known account of the actor, Garrick his name was. The Bishop asked Garrick how he could produce such a magical effect on an audience by the representation of fiction. The actor replied, "Because I recite fiction as if it were truth, and you preach truth as if it were fiction." We need the Jeremiah syndrome, *"His word was in mine heart as a burning fire shut up in my bones"* (Jeremiah 20:9). We don't want heat without light; but where there is light there will be heat in some measure.

The passion in a man's preaching is as a result of his testimony, his own experience of the saving grace of God in Jesus Christ. We'll come shortly to such an example, a man from Gadarene, a man held captive by the powers of hell and loosed by Jesus. When a man knows by experience that he has been plucked from the snare of the devil and the jaws of everlasting torments, when the chains have fallen off, when the power of God unto salvation has gripped his heart, you'll be hard-pressed to shut him up. We have so many silent "Christians" and "churches" today, I fear it is the fruit of what has been or maybe what has not been preached for a long time in our land. God has put his words in the mouths of his people, *"I have put my words in thy mouth"* (Isaiah 51:16). A non-confessing Christian or Church is a misnomer. Where is the heat, the passion, the drive, the fire? The apostle Paul testifies, *"Now then we are ambassadors for Christ, as though God did beseech you by us: we pray you in Christ's stead, be ye reconciled to God"* (2 Corinthians 5:20); and again, *"Knowing, therefore, the terror of the Lord, we persuade men"* (2 Corinthians 5:11). Sadly, I hear what is called preaching today, and it would not persuade me to get out of bed, let alone flee the wrath to come.

A Man from Gadarene

Here is a man who knew beyond anyone that he had been delivered (Luke 8:26-40). He was wild, uncontrollable, except by devils. Jesus came to the rescue, and as a result he wanted to go with Jesus (Luke 8:38). After his experience, wouldn't you? Jesus said, "No" (v39). But what Jesus did not do is to tell him to go and hide away in a church building, nor to do nothing. He gave him his calling, the only one that matters: *"Return to thine own house, and shew how great things God hath done unto thee."* But wait a minute! He's not been to university, or seminary; no man has laid hands on him; and he doesn't even have membership in a church. Plus, he's not been civilised yet: he has just crawled out of the caves! Whatever. Jesus sends him back to his folk. He does not impose too much on this inexperienced street preacher. You know, like, go learn Hebrew and Greek and get a systematic theology into you first. Just, go tell them what great things God has done for you, through Jesus (v39). Just do what you can, is all that was needed. He is to *"shew"* narrate, speak, express repeatedly, what Jesus has done for him (v39). His story was to stir the hearts of all who heard it, to find out more about Jesus. He did, and he did it very well indeed. He went preaching *"throughout the whole city"* (v39)—the Decapolis they called it. *"And he departed and began to publish in Decapolis how great things*

Jesus had done for him: and all men did marvel" (Mark 5:20). The Decapolis was a group of ten cities. The whole region heard about his miraculous deliverance. His calling was preparatory. In time these people will get the gospel in full and saving power. You see, Jesus came back and was *"gladly received"* (v40). This is the same people who in fear bade Jesus depart (v37). The difference?—the street preacher. He had broken up the fallow ground, preparing them for Jesus' return to the region.

My point is a biblical one. One sows, another reaps (John 4:37). It may be your ministry will be just that, to sow the seed, and another will come and reap the harvest; or maybe the other way round. But you must understand that just because you do not see immediate fruit in terms of conversions, it does not necessarily negate the calling or ministry. You must keep on whatever, head down into the wind, and keep on swinging the bat. It is obedience that is required of you. The rest is in the hands of your sovereign Redeemer.

When Two World's Collide

"Now," says Jesus, *"is the judgment of this world."* Which one? There are two. There is the world that is God's and the world that is the world's. The two of them from the beginning have been on a collision course. There is enmity there. God put it there (Genesis 3:15).

There is the world that is God's (John 3:16); the one that he loves, which he has been and is saving, through his Son Jesus Christ. Those who belong to it are those who were given to Jesus Christ by his Father. They and only they will come to Christ, believing in Christ through the preaching of the gospel. This is the world that Christ reconciles to God, *"To wit, that God was in Christ, reconciling the world unto himself, not imputing their trespasses unto them; and hath committed unto us the word of reconciliation"* (2 Corinthians

5:19). Those who belong to this world, Christ by his atoning death brings to God. This is the world that Christ came not to condemn, but to save (John 3:17). It is the world that God loves (John 3:16), God's world. But it is always in collision with man's world.

The world that is man's? It is the world that hated and still hates the disciples of Jesus Christ, *"If the world hate you, ye know that it hated me before it hated you. If ye were of the world, the world would love his own: but because ye are not of the world, but I have chosen you out of the world, therefore the world hateth you"* (John 15:18-19)—especially those who publicly and boldly confess Christ before man's world. We are to *"love not the world, neither the things that are in the world. If any man love the world, the love of the Father is not in him. For all that is in the world, the lust of the flesh, and the lust of the eyes, and the pride of life, is not of the Father, but is of the world. And the world passeth away, and the lust thereof: but he that doeth the will of God abideth for ever"* (1 John 2:15-17). It is a world that is corrupt, ungodly, motivated by sin, and at enmity against God. This world is not the object of God's love, not at all. If you are going to preach the gospel on the street you need to get this firmly embedded in your mind, God does not love all men head for head. The world of man is *"the present evil world"* (Galatians 1:4). It's a swamp, and it's full of the garbage and sewage of man's sin: it is unbelievably stinking, vile, poisonous. And natural man delights to swim in the swamp. It's his pleasure, a delight to him. But what he cannot see is that at the far edge of the swamp there's a drop, a waterfall if you like, that plunges over and down into hell. When the gospel lifeline is thrown to him by the street preacher, he just ignores it. When the preacher cries out with the gospel of salvation to him, he sticks his fingers in his ears. His choice is always to stay in the swamp. Only the power of Christ can rescue him, in a day of his power (Psalm 110:3). But we must warn him, there is coming a day when the swamp will be fully purged by fire, the fiery judgment of God's full and final and fierce wrath. If God has rescued you from the swamp then praise him, but take heed you do not return to it, lest your name be added to that long list of preachers that have brought dishonour and disgrace to the name and cause of Christ.

This is the world Jesus says he does not pray for (John 17:9). This is the world that is already condemned (John 12:31). This is the world of man that is in collision with the kingdom of God in every age—in its power, its wisdom, its science, its industry, its religion and its culture. It operates from the principle of sin, and it can do no other. It is incontinent (2 Timothy 3:3). It cannot keep its enmity in, it must express it. It cannot keep within its hatred for God, its lust for the flesh, adultery, divorce, profanities and vanities. It is a world of strife, unrest and wars. It is the world of man's self-righteousness and man-made religion, where love is spoken of but not known nor practiced. Man's world in the entirety of its culture was judged, condemned by God in Christ before the bar of his justice when they condemned God's Son before its tribunal and executed him. *"Now is the judgment of this world: now shall the prince of this world be cast out"* (John 12:31). Man's world was asked, "What will you do with the Son of God?" With one voice they said, "We will kill him!" Now awaits only the condemnation to be finally executed, after which only God's world will be left. In the meantime, street-preaching man, there are those in that swamp of a world who will be rescued by the faithful preaching of the gospel.

All of us were conceived and born in sin and therefore members of that society of the godless until through grace Christ rescued us from the swamp. He didn't just haul us to the side, but lifted us out, washed and sanctified us—*"such were some you"* (1 Corinthians 6:9). The Lord in his mercy has others yet to be rescued. So who are they? They are those for whom he died. He died only for those who are eternally given to him by the Father. Those given to him by the Father are those whom God has eternally chosen to be his people. Those elect, redeemed in the blood of the cross, are the rescued and the ones yet to be rescued. Go get 'em, preacher man!

Feeding the Church

The street preacher doesn't necessarily see the fruit of his labours. There may be souls added to the kingdom of which he is unaware. Therefore he doesn't get the opportunity to further counsel and guide those people into a sound and true church. However, if that opportunity does arise it is vitally important that he doesn't just leave such people to wander on their own. We have a responsibility to guide the saved and seekers to a suitable church. That might not always be our church, though well and good if it is. So, it behoves us to know of such sound churches to which folks can be directed. This, I say, must be done without compromise. What constitutes a sound church? Just as there are two worlds (see above), there are two churches also—God's and man's. One is called Jerusalem, and the other Sodom and Gomorrah. The latter is the one personified by the Scribes and Pharisees in Jesus' day. It's the one that had him crucified. And today it corrupts and even rejects the Word of God. To knowingly send seekers and converts to such assemblies would be sinful.

So, a true church:

"The marks, by which the true Church is known, are these: if the pure doctrine of the gospel is preached therein; if she maintains the pure administration of the sacraments as instituted by Christ; if church discipline is exercised in punishing of sin: in short, if all things are managed according to the pure Word of God, all things contrary thereto rejected, and Jesus Christ acknowledged as the only Head of the Church. Hereby the true Church may certainly be known, from which no man has a right to separate himself" (Belgic Confession of Faith, Article 29).

And the false church:

"As for the false Church, she ascribes more power and authority to herself and her ordinances than to the Word of God, and will not submit

herself to the yoke of Christ. Neither does she administer the sacraments as appointed by Christ in his Word, but adds to and takes from them, as she thinks proper; she relieth more upon men than upon Christ; and persecutes those, who live holily according to the Word of God, and rebuke her for her errors, covetousness, and idolatry" (Belgic Confession of Faith, Article 29).

These two Churches are easily known and distinguished from each other. The singular mark of an unsound church is its repudiation of the Word of God, with its authority in and over the church. It compromises the faith in giving way to and approving of Sodomite marriage; divorce ever and anon on unbiblical grounds, including remarriage; and it appoints women to its offices in the church.

God has put his words in Zion's mouth (Isaiah 51:16) to fulfil his work, to gather his elect and to harden the reprobate. If, as some churches at this present time, she spits his words out of her mouth and continues to do so, I tell you, wrath will come upon her. So, in mission work of any sort, albeit street preaching, it is imperative that people are fed into true, solid, Reformed churches that are clearly distinguished by bearing the marks of a true church, where the doctrines of grace are taught and the pure gospel is expounded; and, in a day and generation where it seems that just about anything and anyone goes, discipline is applied uncompromisingly and without favour. The preacher himself ought to be a member of such a church and have been sent by such a church and be informed of churches in the locality where he is working, that he may guide people who show a serious interest in the gospel.

Caring & Cautiousness

As you engage in a street ministry you will get the opportunity, doubtless, of encouraging other believers. You'll come across poor souls that have been damaged by church experiences and won't return for love nor money. Seek to bind up their wounds, point and draw them to Christ the great healer. Don't scold. You'll come across back-sliders who find it so hard to return to the Father's house. Encourage them. You'll come across some of the poorest, damaged souls, who will come at you not so much asking for help, but screaming abuse at you. It's only as you respond with the soft answer that they begin to melt and then the tears come and the sorrows come pouring out. Minister Christ to them. The street work is great work. There is nothing like it, believe me, and I still love it after all these years. Then you will come across others, men and women with the same burden for souls as you. You may be allowed to counsel them in the best way forward, though for them not necessarily the same as for you.

Perhaps as your gifts and abilities develop you will be given opportunities to preach in other churches besides your own. Your business there is to encourage, not to scold or correct. That's their pastor's job, not yours. There are other forms of evangelism besides street preaching. Some are called to plant churches. There you also may find some usefulness, in encouraging those engaged in such a work. You may perhaps even be given the chance of instigating someone to start such an endeavour; but having done so you have a responsibility to return often to encourage and strengthen those involved. Whatever the ministry be, it is always about edifying, building up. You live and minister in a world of broken, ruined souls who have already been abused by many others. The work on the street is an opportunity to present them with a ministry that truly offers them with hope, the only hope, Christ. There will be times when you'll be judged as harsh. Well, you must examine yourself. A minister once said to me that when we're criticised, and maybe not for the best intentions, there will always be a grain of truth in it. Don't just ignore it—but in preaching for conviction of sin we're always going to be open to such charges. It is inevitable.

In caring for others you will need to be cautious also. The dangers are many. There is a Devil. He is still busy, and you're on his territory. If he can bring you down he will. Never, never, get yourself alone with the opposite sex other than with your spouse. The path of redemptive history is littered with a large number of men who have fallen in this area. Also, do not even be on your own with other people's children. There are some very evil children, believe me. Your enemy, the Devil, is an expert hunter. He knows his prey, how to bait the hook, set the trap. He knows your weakness— he has been at his business a long, long time. He has studied human nature, and he knows what you're made of. So you need to pay heed to the Saviour's words, *"Watch and pray."* You need day by day the full armour of God. You need to put it on upon your knees. You need protection from unreasonable and wicked men, and ungodly powers and authorities. Every day and every preaching situation is different and the enemy comes in a different route every time. One of the most dangerous times is after great success or victory. Immediately your guard is down. Then he comes in like a lightning bolt to take you down. Be caring but be cautious.

Stipend or Support

I guess something should be said about the street preacher's keep. This also is a difficult issue. If you live in the United Kingdom you could well starve to death. However, it fares somewhat better for the brethren across the Pond. The American Christians do seem to have a bigger heart for street ministry. I have no real experience in other countries so I cannot comment on them. If you're not supported financially by your church then usually a tent-making ministry is the next best option. You could, of course, take employment with a para-church missionary society, but that has a lot of tensions, towing their party line to keep their supporters on board etc. Also, there is not much room for a preacher who has serious Reformed convictions. I only know of one brother in this line of work in these parts who is fully supported by his church. This is exceptional. Financial giving for frontline evangelism is at an all-time low in the British Isles. Over the years I have had to take employment to make ends meet for short periods. I have noticed that some brothers appeal for support through social media outlets. How this works for them in practice I'm not sure. Then some frown upon such practices. But in fairness, if people are not made aware of a Christian worker's genuine need how will they know that there is an opportunity to give. How many would testify, *"If I'd only known, I would've gladly given."* So you have to go with your conscience on that one. I think though that when others are supporting you, whether a church, or individuals, and whether it's regular or one-off giving, that puts a responsibility on you to be a very good steward of that support, to use it carefully, wisely and well.

For this lack of support for street ministry to be rectified there would need to be a serious movement on the part of the Lord, I think, melting the frozen love of Christians to tears of sorrow for a world of ruined sinners. Sadly, they think it's only at special times that God is working. The tendency is to be dismayed and therefore somewhat blinded to the reality of God working just as much in the years of decline, for he is as much responsible for the one as he is for the other. But the street preacher mustn't let himself be dismayed by this state of affairs. It simply should cast him upon the Lord all the more. This will grow his faith to look to the Lord to provide a way for him. The support may not necessarily come from one church, but others within the presbytery or denomination, the strong supporting the weak. I have been quite staggered at how he has provided for me. In times of doubt, I have to keep reminding myself of those former experiences and rebuke myself.

All this said. If a church is sending a man to preach the gospel, albeit on the street, or wherever, are they not duty-bound to support him? I think they are. But what if they can't? The apostle Paul laboured as a tent-maker in Corinth, but that was because of a narrow, critical spirit which was pervasive there. He supported himself so that the gospel wouldn't be hindered there (1 Corinthians

9:12). It is not beneath the dignity of a preacher to engage in manual labour, to drive a truck, or labour on a farm, but it would distract from his preaching ministry to some degree (Matthew 10:10; Luke 10:7; 1 Corinthians 9:14). Though he is a street preacher his needs are no different to that of others. Maybe he has a family to keep. He needs to be buying books constantly (not cheap either), and present himself in a neat and tidy appearance (especially on the street). Appearance is not a matter of small importance. I don't think the street preacher needs to dress as he would if he were preaching in his church. In that situation he should be dressed in his very best, but on the street he should be dressed for the street. That doesn't mean anything goes, but he should be clean, tidy, and smartly attired, though casually so; but, please, not religious garb. We need to remember who it is we are representing at all times.

Privilege & Pride

There has always been and I think still is today, an awful pride and selfishness in the church. Paul addresses this in the New Testament, speaking to the Corinthians (1 Corinthians 1:26-31). He speaks of the seriousness and urgency of the gospel ministry over against the squabbling selfishness and pride of the Corinthian Christians. He could do so today in many places. He reminds them that they were just ordinary people, nothing special, not nobles, not high-fliers. You see whatever your station is, what your gifts are, and everything you've got, except your sin, is from God. So what place is there for pride (1 Corinthians 6:9ff)? What have you got that you didn't receive? So if God uses you in any capacity at all you need to remind yourself that it was God's doing not yours and the glory is his too, not yours. It's this attitude alone that will keep you in a place of usefulness. Who put you in Christ? God did. He gave you light, life and liberty; he called you. If you don't keep yourself beneath the shadow of the cross day by day you will end up spiritually useless.

In the light of that cross let it pour utter contempt on all your pride. *"I will not boast in anything, no gifts, no power, no wisdom; but I will boast in Jesus Christ, His death and resurrection"* (S. Townsend).

Much hardness and bitterness can enter the soul of the street preacher as a result of the rejection and hostility that he encounters, but this must be dealt with in the same way as any pride that would creep in—by nailing it to the cross. There will be fellow preachers who will reject you, and pastors who ought to know better will look down theological noses at you. There will be others of your fraternity who will criticise you (normally behind your back), and perhaps even disown you. You may incur trouble with the authorities, be arrested, arraigned and jailed for preaching the gospel. Other Christians will disown you. They will say it was your foolish fault. If ever a church needed serious suffering it's the church in the West today, for that's the only thing that will purge the church of her self-righteous respectability and bring God's true people together, showing just exactly how small she is, a tiny flock. But in the meantime, you must continue in your course doing what God has called you to do. *"If God be for us, who can be against us* (Romans 8:31)? So go to it.

The Preacher's Devotion

The subject of devotion cannot be mentioned without our minds turning to the subject of prayer. The sheer discipline of Jesus is amazing (Mark 1:35-39). In spite of the long hard day, he is up very early (v35), engaging in private prayer. His praying, as recorded (Luke 3.21; 5.16; 6.12; 9.18; 11.1; Matthew 11.25; John 11.41 17.1), always seems connected to something of significance in his ministry. In this particular instance, it is his resolve to preach the gospel of the kingdom. As a man, Jesus was dependent upon his Father in all things, and it was in this way he prayed and expressed his obedient love and perfect unison with his Father. He was in constant communication with his Father, bringing his work and ministry, for which the Father had sent him and given him to do, before that same Father. The Son of God was sinless, but as a man, he was kept so by the regular use of the means of grace, not in the neglect of them.

One of our biggest problems today is that we live at a hundred miles an hour, so fast, too fast. We need to slow down, and find a quiet deserted place for solitary self-examination and meditation upon the being and the Word of God. There can be too much preaching and hearing with us, but not enough of this solitary, contemplative prayer life; and the more work you have to do, the more you need to pray. The disciples finding the Lord missing went in search of him (v36). That's a good thing to do as well. But they were not the only ones (v37). The people from the previous evening no doubt, spread the word about Jesus and his ministry, and drew even more people to him. They did not want him to leave the area (Luke 4.42), but Jesus cannot accede to their request, as he has pressing business (Mark 1.14-15, 38)—preaching in the next towns. This verse ought to silence forever and ever those who complain about preaching. The fact that the eternal Son of God himself undertook the office of a preacher is enough to tell us it is a valuable means of grace.

Preaching is God's principal instrument in awakening sinners and edifying Christians. The kingdom of God is built and established by preaching. The Lord tells us himself here, that his work, his mission, was, through the means of this gospel preaching, to draw people to repentance and faith, bringing them under the blessed rule of himself, King Jesus. The preaching of God's Word is essential, a must, and the Church has a moral obligation to preach. It was for this reason Jesus was sent, commissioned by his Father, and he says to his Church in the very same way, *"even so send I you"* (John 20.21). The great need of the day is gospel preaching churches, exposing the Word of God to the hearts and minds of people, not simply giving the ABC's of the gospel, but the thorough, serious and thoughtful proclamation of the whole counsel of God. But, get this, it must be a prayer-soaked ministry. We may say we preach overmuch, and maybe so, but none shall ever say they spent too much time praying.

Prayer *is* the work. It is the hardest work of all. The intent of praying is not to change God or his mind or to twist his arm to do such and such a thing that we desire. No, it is designed to change us, to bring us to a further and deeper submission to him and his will; to change us, not God; to change our wills, not God's.

The street preacher in every age needs to be clothed upon with the whole armour of God (Ephesians 6:11ff). This need is becoming increasingly vital in these days, which I believe to be the beginning of the last days. Each piece must be lovingly and carefully put on, suited and booted, as a good soldier prepared for battle. The hostility is on the increase. Here in the United Kingdom, we have had street preachers facing violence. One pastor who was violated, suffered concussion; others have had equipment broken and destroyed—so prayerfully clothing oneself in God's armour is vital. We must be ready to *"endure hardship as a good soldier of Jesus Christ"* (2 Timothy 2:3). You have to deal with enemies without and within. You are not going to be loved, but criticised, even by Christians. Dealing with carnal worshippers can be thorny, to say the least. As you confront people regarding sin, reproving works of darkness, you will not be thanked for it. As you stand firm on the sovereignty of the Word of God you will face opposition. The best preparation for all such enmity is on your knees before you hit the street and to be loaded with the Holy Spirit's advice: *"Wherefore take unto you the whole armour of God, that ye may be able to withstand in the evil day, and having done all, to stand. Stand therefore, having your loins girt about with truth, and having on the breastplate of righteousness; And your feet shod with the preparation of the gospel of peace; Above all, taking the shield of faith, wherewith ye shall be able to quench all the fiery darts of the wicked. And take the helmet of salvation, and the sword of the Spirit, which is the word of God: Praying always with all prayer and supplication in the Spirit, and watching thereunto with all perseverance and supplication for all saints"* (Ephesians 6:13-18).

The exhortation to keep ourselves in the love of God (Jude 21) is a very important one and especially so in the context of our present subject. Perhaps this should have been stated earlier, and we need to say something about it. The question, of course, is how do we keep ourselves in the love of God? We do so by using every means which love commands, and avoiding all things that love forbids. The latter is not legalism. The world talks about love today, but what they speak of is mere emotion. It is not founded, grounded, in Divine love. It is simply a notion in the head. They are strangers to the constraints of love. To keep ourselves in the love of God is to meditate upon his love to us, daily. It is knowing, believing, the love that God has for us. He demonstrated that love in giving his only begotten Son for us, to atone by his precious blood. What are we doing here, but preaching to ourselves, before we preach to others? In the gospel, we preach that God revealed his love to us, so our great need before any form of service is to keep our souls in and under a lively sense of this Divine love.

But that also means keeping ourselves from the worldly, fleshly lusts that war against our souls, from carnal indulgences and sensual gratifications. For the love of God and his mercies to us in Christ, and for our very soul's sake, we must abstain from them. As bad food will impair your bodily health, these indulgences will impair the health of your soul. They will rob your soul of its peace and dampen the warm sense of God's love. *"Consider your ways"* (Haggai 1:5), says the prophet. What is life without his love? What joy can be compared with this, to serve and to please the Lord always? So we must keep ourselves in the Word of God daily, in praying, and in fasting. We must use of the special means of grace for ourselves, the preaching of God's Word, getting under good solid, sound preaching, week by week. Then there is the fellowship of God's people, especially other gospel preachers. Maybe in the providence of God you are working alone most of the time, a very lonely and difficult pathway. Perhaps you need to travel now and again to get with other brothers, for mutual encouragement. We need the fellowship of all Christians, but the fraternity of street preachers is a very special fellowship. Nobody knows the heartaches, the pitfalls and the enjoyments of street preaching as they do. It does us a world of good to be together sometimes at least. We sharpen, quicken and strengthen one another. But, whatever it takes, *"keep yourselves in the love of God"* (Jude 21).

Finally, if God has called you to preach his Word, his calling is without repentance (Romans 11:29). It is irrevocable—for life. You take it up and do not lay it down. It demands your absolute commitment (2 Corinthians 5:14; John 9:4). You must always be willing to preach although you may not feel like it (1 Corinthians 9:16-17), persevering although the way is hard, through wind and rain, good times and bad, discouragements and encouragements (2 Timothy 4:1-6)—as sanctified, set apart for this great gospel work (Romans 1:1).

Appendix 1

What is the Reformed Faith?

What do Reformed Christians believe about doctrine, salvation, the Bible and God's covenant of Grace?

The Holy Scriptures

We are blessed with an accurate and authoritative Bible. Therefore, our appeal is always and ever to the testimony of Scripture, and here we stand or fall. *"To the law and to the testimony: if they speak not according to this word, it is because there is no light in them"* (Isaiah 8:20). What we hold to and what we proclaim is what the Bible says. We and our neighbour (all we come in contact with) need, as the Lord Jesus commands, to *"search the scriptures; for in them ye think ye have eternal life: and they are they which testify of me"* (John 5:39). It is there that Christ is to be found, not in all creation, the universe, the world, in man himself or his reason. By what means is God made known to us?

"We know him by two means: first, by the creation, preservation and government of the universe; which is before our eyes as a most elegant book, wherein all creatures, great and small, are as so many

characters leading us to contemplate the invisible things of God, namely, his power and divinity, as the apostle Paul saith, (Romans 1:20). All which things are sufficient to convince men, and leave them without excuse. Secondly, he makes himself more clearly and fully known to us by his holy and divine Word, that is to say, as far as is necessary for us to know in this life, to his glory and our salvation" (Belgic Confession of Faith, Article 2).

"Although the light of nature, and the works of creation and providence, do so far manifest the goodness, wisdom, and power of God, as to leave men inexcusable; yet are they not sufficient to give that knowledge of God, and of his will, which is necessary unto salvation; therefore it pleased the Lord, at sundry times, and in divers manners, to reveal himself, and to declare that his will unto his Church; and afterwards, for the better preserving and propagating of the truth, and for the more sure establishment and comfort of the Church against the corruption of the flesh, and the malice of Satan and of the world, to commit the same wholly unto writing; which maketh the holy Scripture to be most necessary; those former ways of God's revealing his will unto his people being now ceased" (Westminster Confession of Faith, 1:1).

God's Eternal Decree

We maintain that God is sovereign, that he has decreed and is the first cause of all things. It is he who has created the universe and all in it (in six literal days) (Genesis 1) and he is the one by whom all things consist, i.e., are upheld (Colossians 1:17). All moral, rational creatures are under his sovereign sway. He has decreed to save some (his elect) (Ephesians 1:4), but that others should be punished in hell for their sins (Romans 9:22). We hold without swerving this great biblical truth of the sovereignty of God. (Recommended reading: *The Sovereignty of God*, by A. W. Pink).

"God from all eternity did, by the most wise and holy counsel of his own will, freely and unchangeably ordain whatsoever comes to pass;

yet so as thereby neither is God the author of sin, nor is violence offered to the will of the creatures, nor is the liberty or contingency of second causes taken away, but rather established" (Westminster Confession of Faith, 3:1).

God's Covenant of Grace

The Bible reveals that God's gracious covenant is unilateral, being established by God himself directly (Genesis 15:17-18). That is to say, it is not a contract or agreement between two parties. It is formed, established and maintained by God. It is both unbreakable and inviolable, through all the business of life and into all eternity (Genesis 17:7). God's covenant of grace is established in the line of believers and their seed (Genesis 17:7; Acts 2:39). That does not mean that all the children of believers are saved, *"As it is written, Jacob have I loved, but Esau have I hated"* (Romans 9:13). Others outside of the line of generations are sovereignly brought into the covenant of grace.

"Man by his fall having made himself incapable of life by that covenant, the Lord was pleased to make a second, commonly called the covenant of grace: wherein he freely offered unto sinners life and salvation by Jesus Christ, requiring of them faith in him that they may be saved and promising to give unto all those that are ordained unto life his Holy Spirit, to make them willing and able to believe" (Westminster Confession of Faith, 7:3).

The Five Points

Of Calvinism, as they are known. They are not an exhaustive expression of what is meant either by Calvinism or the Reformed Faith. They express the distinction between the Reformation's biblical position and that of the heresy of Arminianism. The acrostic TULIP is generally used to denote it.

T is for *"Total Depravity."* Man's condition in sin, as he is both conceived and born (Psalm 51:5; Romans 1:18-32). Wanting for any good whatsoever (Romans 3:10-18). Spiritually dead in his trespasses and sins, unable to accomplish any spiritual reformation himself (Romans 5:6).

U is for *"Unconditional Election."* Those whom God saves are saved as a result of God's election of grace (Romans 11:5). This election took place before God created the universe and mankind. We were not present; it was before anyone did anything good or bad. God chose his people, not an arbitrary number, but chose himself a Church. Election is the source and foundation of the covenant of grace. Those whom God has predestinated (elected) to eternal life shall be saved (Ephesians 1:4-5).

L is for *"Limited Atonement."* The atoning death of Jesus Christ God's Son was not for all men, head for head, but only for the elect—those given to Jesus before the foundation of the world (John 17:9). He died for his people (Matthew 1:21), his sheep (John 10:11) only.

I is for *"Irresistible Grace."* None come to Christ unless drawn of the Father (John 6:44), but those who are drawn come, irresistibly. They are made willing in a day of Christ's power (Psalm 110:3). There is a time was they are not willing (John 5:40), but when Christ calls, just as he called dead Lazarus from the tomb (John 11:43), the dead sinner comes to him willingly.

P is for *"Perseverance of the Saints."* Those chosen in Christ, drawn of the Father, regenerated by the Holy Ghost, are also kept by the power of God (1 Peter 1:5). Preserved in the hand of the Father and the Son (John 10:28-29). The work of God in them can never be undone; they are justified unto all eternity. They shall never perish. They are as safe as safe can be.

The Law of God

The law is not antithetical to grace, as some would have us to believe. *"Wherefore the law is holy, and the commandment holy, and just, and good"* (Romans 7:12). It is God's perfect rule for us, pre-fall and post-fall (James 1:25). It is our infallible guide (Deuteronomy 5:32). In regeneration God renews our wills, giving to them new qualities, so enabling us to walk in his statutes (Ezekiel 36:25-27). He writes the law upon our hearts (Hebrews 10:16). The law is not given to save us; it cannot give us life, love or liberty, only the gospel can do that. The law is our schoolmaster, to teach us the sinfulness of our sin, the absolute holiness of God and it directs us to Christ for salvation (Galatians 3:24). Salvation is in Christ alone (John 14:6; Acts 4:12; Romans 8:3). The ceremonial laws are now abrogated under the New Testament.

"God gave to Adam a law, as a covenant of works, by which he bound him and all his posterity to personal, entire, exact, and perpetual obedience; promised life upon the fulfilling, and threatened death upon the breach of it; and endued him with power and ability to keep it."

"This law, after his fall, continued to be a perfect rule of righteousness; and, as such, was delivered by God upon mount Sinai in ten commandments, and written in two tables; the first four commandments containing our duty towards God, and the other six our duty to man" (Westminster Confession of Faith, 9:1-2).

Religious Worship

To worship God, to glorify and enjoy him, is the very purpose for which we were made and for which we are saved. Thankfully God has not left us to wonder how this is to be accomplished. He has given us his revelation, his Word, the Bible, to that end. Worship is to be according to God's revealed Word. If it is not commanded it is not permitted; if it is declared unacceptable then it is forbidden.

True worship of God is opposed to the free for all we see in many so-called churches today. The commandments of men do not dictate Christian worship (Matthew 15:9). God does not desire our smart modern ideas of what constitutes worship (Act 17:25). He is to be worshipped as he commands, *"God is a Spirit: and they that worship him must worship him in spirit and in truth"* (John 4:24). God is God, utterly holy, all he does is holy, and we are to be actuated by both his commandment and his promise: to fear him (Jeremiah 10:7); to love him (Psalm 31:23); and to trust and serve him with integrity and loyalty (Psalm 62:8; Joshua 24:14).

"The light of nature showeth that there is a God, who hath lordship and sovereignty over all; is good, and doeth good unto all; and is therefore to be feared, loved, praised, called upon, trusted in, and served with all the heart, and with all the soul, and with all the might. But the acceptable way of worshipping the true God is instituted by himself, and so limited to his own revealed will, that he may not be worshipped according to the imaginations and devices of men, or the suggestions of Satan, under any visible representations or any other way not prescribed in the Holy Scripture" (Westminster Confession of Faith 21:1).

Of Mission

In accordance with the express command of our Lord Jesus Christ, *"Go ye therefore, and teach all nations, baptising them in the name of the Father, and of the Son, and of the Holy Ghost: Teaching them to observe all things whatsoever I have commanded you: and, lo, I am with you alway, even unto the end of the world. Amen"* (Matthew 28:19-20), we go, into *all* the world, preaching Christ indiscriminately to all men who will hear. The preaching of God's Word is the especial means appointed by God for this task: *"For Christ sent me not to baptise, but to preach the gospel: not with wisdom of words, lest the cross of Christ should be made of none effect. For the preaching of the cross is to them that perish foolishness; but unto us which are saved it is the power of God"* (1 Corinthians 1:17-18). God only knows those who are his. The preaching of the gospel is ever a two-edged sword, *"for we are unto God a sweet savour of Christ, in them that are saved, and in them that perish: To the one we are the savour of death unto death; and to the other the savour of life unto life. And who is sufficient for these things"* (2 Corinthians 2:15-16).

"Q. 155. How is the Word made effectual to salvation?
A. The Spirit of God maketh the reading, but especially the preaching of the Word, an effectual means of enlightening, convincing, and humbling sinners; of driving them out of themselves, and drawing them unto Christ; of conforming them to his image, and subduing them to his will; of strengthening them against temptations and corruptions; of building them up in grace, and establishing their hearts in holiness and comfort through faith unto salvation" (Westminster Larger Catechism, Q & A 155).

After Death

Death is not a state of non-being. Death is sin's wages (Romans 6:23). It has been appointed for all: *"As it is appointed unto men once to die, but after this the judgment"* (Hebrews 9:27). The righteous await redemption, the wicked and unbelieving are reserved for judgment. The misery of the lost is portrayed by the Lord Jesus in his account of the rich man and Lazarus the beggar (Luke 16:20-31). The Bible, Holy Scripture makes no mention of a place called purgatory as an in-between state after death, The only two destinations are heaven and hell. Surely we are to take heed, be warned. And surely if we have any love in our hearts for our neighbour we will clearly and sharply warn him of such awaiting danger.

"The bodies of men, after death, return to dust, and see corruption; but their souls (which neither die nor sleep), having an immortal subsistence, immediately return to God who gave them. The souls of

the righteous, being then made perfect in holiness, are received into the highest heavens, where they behold the face of God in light and glory, waiting for the full redemption of their bodies: and the souls of the wicked are cast into hell, where they remain in torments and utter darkness, reserved to the judgment of the great day. Besides these two places for souls separated from their bodies, the Scripture acknowledgeth none" (Westminster Confession of Faith, 32:1).

The Last Judgment

The day has been appointed, and the Judge has been appointed (Acts 17:31). Judge Jesus has already been given the power of judgment (John 5:22, 27). Therefore, it is appropriate that he should be the one who carries out the final tribunal. The justice will be like no human court or judiciary. It will be perfectly righteous. God hates and abhors all sin. He is angry with the wicked every day (Psalm 7:11). In that day men will become either an object of God's wrath for all eternity or an object God's admiration for all eternity. For you, which will it be? Will Christ be your Advocate in that courtroom? Will he say, "Depart from me," or will he say, "Come?"

"*God hath appointed a day wherein he will judge the world in righteousness by Jesus Christ, to whom all power and judgment is given of the Father. In which day, not only the apostate angels shall be judged, but likewise all persons, that have lived upon earth, shall appear before the tribunal of Christ, to give an account of their thoughts, words, and deeds; and to receive according to what they have done in the body, whether good or evil*" (Westminster Confession of Faith, 33:1).

Conclusion

This is the truth, albeit but a summary, of the Reformed Faith. Much, much more could be said. This is the truth that refutes all other ways to God (Acts 4:12). It declares the God of Scripture to be the only true and living God. The gods of the world religions are vain idols. The Reformed Faith refutes the false man-made religions of an apostate world: of Roman Catholicism, of apostate Christianity, the god of free-will, of Arminianism, of Pentecostalism, and of the Charismatics. The Reformed Faith is just another way of saying what the Bible, God's Word, says. It declares the God we are called and sent to proclaim faithfully to all men without distinction. As with all else about our salvation, we must continue as instructed by God's Word. *"Study to shew thyself approved unto God, a workman that needeth not to be ashamed, rightly dividing the word of truth"* (2 Timothy 2:15). *"Let every man be fully persuaded in his own mind"* (Romans 14:5). Study, dig deep and learn as Scripture itself urges us to do, and pray for God to *"open your eyes, that you may behold wondrous things out of his word"* (Psalm 119:18).

Appendix 2

Examples of Street Sermon Outlines

'Repent Ye' (Acts 3:19)

1. <u>The Nature of Sin</u>: v19

    a) A Knowledge of Sin
    b) A Conviction of Sin
    c) A Sorrow for Sin
    d) A Self-Loathing for Sin
    e) A Confessing & Turning From Sin

2. <u>The Evidences of Repentance</u>: v19

    a) A Right State of Mind
    b) A Spiritual Conversion
    c) An Obedience to the Truth
    d) A Union with Christ by Faith

3. <u>The Necessity of Repentance</u>: v19)

    a) Needful for a Right State of Mind
    b) Needful for God's Approval
    c) Needful for Own Peace
    d) Needful for Entrance to Heaven

'The Engrafted Word' (James 1:21)

1. <u>The Reception of the Word</u>: (v21)

   a) Without the Word Men Perish
   b) Will of God Some are Saved
   c) Word Begets Those Who are Saved
   d) Man Rejects the Word Willfully because it's God's

2. <u>The Rejecters of the Word</u>: v21

   a) Hear Not Because Not of God
   b) Hear Not Because Heart's Hardened
   c) Word's Content is Person of Christ
   d) Word's Work is to Beget Children of God
   e) Word of Man's Ineffective/Impotent.

3. <u>The Results of the Engrafted Word</u>: v21

   a) Word of Truth Saves
   b) Word Saves from Sin
   c) Word's Planted by God via Preaching
   d) Word Never Returns Void
   e) Word Planted Transforms Life

'What the Law Could Not Do' (Romans 8:34)

1. <u>The Inefficiency of the Law</u>: v3f

   a) It Cannot Pardon the Guilty
   b) It Cannot Remove Impurity of Soul
   c) It Cannot Heal the Alienation from God
   d) It Cannot Prevent the Infliction of the Penalty

2. **The Instituted Means:** v3f

    a) The Author is God
    b) The Agent is His Son
    c) The Commission is to Save
    d) The Work Given to Condemn Sin in the Flesh

3. **The Intention in Sending Jesus:** v3f

    a) Sinners be Justified from All Things
    b) Sinners Declared Truly Righteous
    c) Sinners Turned From Idols to God

'The Power That Brings Salvation' (Romans 1:16)

1. **The Great Instrument:** v16

    a) Law Holds Captive - Gospel Satisfies its Claims
    b) Satan Holds Captive - Gospel Destroys His Works
    c) Sin Holds Captive - Person of Christ Liberates
    d) Lie Holds Captive - Truth Gospel Conquers

2. **The Gracious Operation:** v16

    a) Gospel Awakens & Converts Sinners
    b) Gospel Justifies Sinners before God
    c) Gospel Transforms, Makes Bad Good
    d) Gospel Preserves Those it Saves
    e) Gospel Brings Believers to Glory

'Death' (Psalm 39:4)

1. **The End of All Men:** v4

    a) End of All Temporal Concerns

b) End All Earthly Relations
   c) End of Man's Probation/Stewardship
   d) End of All Man's Exertions

2. <u>The End Men Forget</u>: v4

   a) Because it's Disagreeable
   b) Because they're Absorbed with Earthly Things
   c) Because Satan Blinds Them

3. <u>The End Desirable</u>: v4

   a) Prayerfully Remember Your End
   b) Pray God to Save & Sanctify You
   c) Pray for Repentance & Faith
   d) Pray to be Ready for Death

'The Death of the Righteous' (Numbers 23:10)

1. <u>The Character of the Righteous</u>: v10

   a) He's Justified
   b) He's Regenerated
   c) He's Sanctified
   d) He's Practically Obedient

2. <u>The Fruit of Righteous</u>: v10

   a) He Dies Under God's Immediate Direction
   b) He Dies in State of Gracious Security
   c) He Dies in Ecstasy & Triumph
   d) He Dies Entering into Life & Immortality

3. <u>The Desire Itself is Insufficient</u>: v10

   a) Needs Personal Faith Working by Love
   b) Needs Preparation for Dying
   c) Needs Submission to God's Will

'The Repentant Heart' (Luke 13:3)

1. <u>The Nature of Repentance</u>: v3

   a) It's Sorrow for Sin
   b) It's Hatred of Sin
   c) It's Forsaking Sin

2. <u>The Cause of Repentance</u>: v3

   a) It's God
   b) It's God's Grace
   c) It's Through God's Word
   d) It's Through Operations of the Spirit

3. <u>The Necessity of Repentance</u>: v3

   a) Because All Are Sinners
   b) Because No Communion with God Without it
   c) Because Eternally Lost if Live & Die in Sin

Appendix 3

A Brief Account of the Street Preacher's Testimony

I was born in the city of Glasgow in 1944 in the district of Langside. The city's motto back then was *"Let Glasgow Flourish by the Preaching of His Word and the Praising of His Name."* Sadly, Glasgow no longer flourishes. That's where I grew up. Our church life was with the Church of Scotland, also sadly in decline both spiritually and morally. My father's business collapsed and he did a runner, leaving my mother, sister and myself to fend for ourselves. I would have been about nine years of age then. Unknown to me at the time, my mother was dying of cancer. I think it was because of this that she started taking us to the meetings at the "Tent Hall" in Glasgow. The "Tent Hall" was begun back in the late 1800's, partly through the influence of D.L. Moody and others. It was renowned for its Sunday night evangelistic meetings. At the age of nine, going on a ten, I couldn't have told what the difference was, but I knew this wasn't the Church of Scotland. These men were serious. They meant business, and there was a whole different level to their preaching and singing. I understand now, of course, that there was gospel life there. Then in 1953, Dr Billy Graham came to Glasgow, and he preached at the Kelvin Hall. My mother took us to hear Dr Graham. It seems obvious to me now that my mother was looking for something or someone. Whether she actually found the Saviour, or rather he found her, I can't be certain, but I like to think so.

With my mother's departure from this world, my sister and I moved over to the north side of Glasgow, to the district of Springburn, to live with my grandparents. The religion continued with the Church of Scotland, at Cowlairs Parish Church. I attended the Boys Brigade, Sunday School, and of course Church on the Sunday. My grandparents, as far as I know, didn't know the Lord. They were traditionally religious, raised that way in the north of Scotland, and lived out their lives that way. They were very respectable, and diligent in their church attendance. My grandfather was a member of the Kirk Session. All that said, my sister and I owe them a tremendous debt. They very kindly took us in and raised us the rest of the way—this, of course, having already raised four children of their own, and that through the years of the Second World War. They lived through the German blitz of Glasgow's Clydeside where many of our warships were built in those trying times. I recall seeing tears well up in my Granny's eyes when she heard the sound of an aeroplane. My sister and I would have ended up in an orphanage but for their sacrificial kindness.

I left school at the age of fifteen and started an apprenticeship on the Clydeside, in Govan on the edge of the river Clyde. At the age of almost eighteen, I joined the Air Force. I travelled around the world, Singapore, Persian Gulf, Cyprus, Germany as well as the United Kingdom. My drinking career had already begun before leaving Glasgow and that increased as the years progressed. I think a heavy drinking culture goes with military service in just about any country in any age.

It was during this time that my sister had become a Christian. A girl from a Plymouth Brethren assembly had moved in next door back in Springburn. She started to witness to my sister, Margaret, much to her indignation. My sister was still with the Church of

Scotland, and was a Sunday School teacher. Margaret eventually concluded that this girl believed the Bible, but she did not. As she was teaching it to children, her conclusion was that it was hypocrisy, so she quit the Sunday School, the Church, all of it. The minister, the Kirk Session, and everyone are going ballistic, but she won't have it any other way. She began attending meetings with Isobel, her new neighbour. She attended the Tron Church in Glasgow city center, back when Rev George Duncan was the minister. He preached on the occasion of her conversion on the text, *"My Spirit shall not always strive with man"* (Genesis 6:3).

Meanwhile, I'm drinking my way around the world, on a fifteen-year engagement in the Royal Air Force. I was demobbed in 1975, at the age of thirty-one. Just a month after I left the Air Force, while I was working as a truck driver, I was involved in an accident on the M1 motorway in Northamptonshire, England. There was a spillage of nitric acid, which I fell into. I was taken first of all to a local hospital where the doctor took one look at me and said, "What can I do with that? Get him out of here." They took me to Stoke Mandeville, to a specialist burns unit. When the ambulance arrived at the Burns Unit a team of medics were all lined up waiting. The leading doctor railed at the nurse in the ambulance, "What's he doing still awake?" he said. She replied, "He's had enough to knock out an elephant, but he won't go." If I was going to die I wanted to be around when it happened. The first thing they did was to plunge me in an alkaline bath because the acid was still working. Then there were months and months of operations, skin grafts. They took all the skin of my left leg and grafted it on to my back where most of the damage was. When they took me into that hospital I prayed for the first time since I was a child. I said, "God, if you give me another chance I promise you I'll be a different man." They put me back together, after months of operations and the most excruciating pain. When I was leaving the hospital the surgeon said to me that as a result of the trauma my body had been through, I'd probably experience a measure of depression. The depression was horrendous, and I forgot all about the prayer.

In trying to fight the depression, my marriage was breaking apart. I tried to face it the only way I knew, with more drink. And the more I drank the more depressed I became. There followed five years of descent into a very dark place where I just could not have cared whether I lived or died. I'm looking at my life, and all the brokenness behind me and I'm thinking, "Is this as good as it gets? Is this all that there is?"

It was at this time that I picked up this book that my sister had given me some eight years previous, while I was still in the Air Force. For some reason I'd always kept it though I wasn't interested. I'd pick it up now and again, read a bit and laugh. I'd think, 'Yeah, this is okay for you Margaret, but it's not for me.' But now here I am reading it properly. It was written by an American pastor. He was saying that every trouble you've faced in your life has come from one source, your own sinful heart. He spoke about a man who had lost his business, his home, and his wife and kids because of his drinking problem; but Jesus had saved him. His life was transformed, and all was back on track, so to speak. Any thought I would have had about Jesus, I think, would have been equated with my Church of Scotland upbringing. He was somebody for nice respectable people, not for drunken truck drivers. But there was something that struck a chord in my mind. The pastor said, "No, it's not like that. Jesus said, I didn't come to call the righteous, but sinners to repentance." And so for the first time in my life, I was beginning to see myself as a sinner. I saw what the issue was, sin. Now, five years on from the last time I prayed, I prayed again. I said, "Jesus, I don't know if you are there or if I believe this stuff, but this man says you can change people's lives, so I'm asking you to change mine.

That was nearly forty years ago now but it seems like just yesterday. There were no flashing lights or ringing bells. But as the days wore on, I started to read the other book Margaret had given me. It was a copy of the New Testament. It was the Good News version, not long out then (I still have it on my shelf). I even took it to work with me. The thing was alive! I couldn't leave it alone. This Jesus, he knows me, my thoughts, and he is ahead of me every step of the way. As I went on, many things began to change. People I was associated with no longer did. It wasn't so much that I cut off from them. It was they cut off from me. Things I did, places I went, felt unclean, no longer acceptable.

There were addictions—not just to the alcohol, but to cigarettes, the language, the blasphemy, all which were once a part of normal life—which the Lord took away. His grace was just amazing. I went from depression to extreme joy. I used to, in my pre-converted days come up to Glasgow to visit my sister and her husband Billy. Maybe the night before, I'd have a drink. At the breakfast table the morning after, not feeling my brightest, I'd look across the table at Billy who had a smile from ear to ear. I'd think, 'How can anybody be that happy first thing in the morning?' Now I know! I was filled with an insatiable appetite for God's Word.

I was attending a Brethren Assembly to begin with. They were Arminian in their theology, but I didn't understand that then. I started doing Bible correspondence courses with the Bible Training Institute in Glasgow. I wanted to tell the whole world about this person Jesus but didn't know how to. A man from the Birmingham City Mission came to our church on one occasion. He told us about the work that they did, how they got on a soapbox and preached the gospel in the city center, and went around doors telling people the gospel. It was an epiphany, the light came on. This is what I'd been looking for! I was invited down to Birmingham to join them on Saturdays, and that was my first introduction to street preaching. So I began a witness of my own in my town of Stafford. One or two people were converted early on in those days.

But the church situation began to slide. We had a visit to the town from a leading Anglican Charismatic leader. He was not only charismatic but extremely ecumenical. As a result of this, a conflict arose between me and our elders. It was a real struggle. My thinking was, 'How can I a young Christian be right and these guys who've been on the road a long time be wrong?' Eventually, the church invited a Roman Catholic priest to come and minister, and that was the final straw for me. I had to leave and take my family with me. I had visited every one of the elders before leaving, and they all of them, assured me it wouldn't happen, but it did.

We joined an evangelical church further north, in the town of Stoke-On-Trent. It was from there shortly after that I became a church officer and was sent into the work of the Open-Air Mission. I was with them for eight years. It was during this time that I started to do the theological course at Bryntirion, in South Wales. It was a college and course set up by Martin Lloyd-Jones to assist aspiring preachers. I was taught by some lovely and godly men: Graham Harrison, Derek Swan, Howell Jones. I loved that course and learned a lot. It was shortly after that that I was called into pastoral work, doing about eighteen years in all, in different parts of the country. If I'm honest I never enjoyed it as much as I've enjoyed the work on the street. I believe that's what the Lord called me to. The last was the best, a little rural country chapel with just a few folks on board, but we had nigh on ten lovely years there, and enjoyed every minute of it. It sadly petered out in the end. The community around was very affluent, people with so much I guess that they could see no need of God in their lives. But they were left without any excuse, as we took the gospel to them.

So people ask me now, "Oh, so you're retired?" "No," is the short answer. Not quite sure what that word means. For the last five years, I've been back on the street (not that I ever left it). I've been to so far-flung places—Jamaica, different parts of the USA, to Albania, and Ukraine—with the gospel, not to mention all around the UK as well. I have a circuit here in my home county of Staffordshire, with five towns that I visit on the same day each week at the same time. I've been doing this for many years, even when I was in pastoral ministry. As I write this I've just turned seventy-five. Even the writing of this book is a new venture in ministry. My hope and prayer are that the Lord will use this to inspire, encourage and raise an army of street preachers around the world; that God would be glorified through the preaching of his Word and the praising of his name; and that many precious souls would be added to the kingdom of his dear Son. Meanwhile, the work continues. The Lord called me to preach the gospel, so I'll stop when he tells me to stop or when he calls me home.

> I love the Lord, because my voice
> and prayers he did hear.
> I, while I live, will call on him,
> who bowed to me his ear.
>
> God merciful and righteous is,
> yea, gracious is our Lord.
> God saves the meek: I was brought low,
> he did me help afford.
>
> O thou my soul, do thou return
> unto thy quiet rest;
> For largely, lo, the Lord to thee
> his bounty hath expressed.
>
> For my distressed soul from death
> delivered was by thee:
> Thou didst my mourning eyes from tears,
> my feet from falling, free.
>
> What shall I render to the Lord
> for all his gifts to me?
> I'll of salvation take the cup,
> on God's name will I call.

(Scottish Psalter 116:1-2, 5-8, 12-13).

Soli Deo Gloria

(Jimmy Hamilton aka The Street Preacher)

The author is a Reformed, Presbyterian, Evangelical minister at present working in North Staffordshire in the UK, preaching the gospel in and around the North Staffordshire area. He was, until approximately five years ago, the minister of Fole Reformed Presbyterian Chapel. He is now a member of Partick Free Church of Scotland (Continuing) in Glasgow is working as an itinerant missionary. He also travels more widely, preaching in some of the towns and cities throughout the country and world, including Jamaica, Ukraine, Malta, Albania and the USA. He also preaches in many congregations at home and abroad.

Lightning Source UK Ltd.
Milton Keynes UK
UKHW010723221219
355797UK00009B/4/P